www.trafford.com

North America & international
toll-free: 1 888 232 4444 (USA & Canada)
phone: 250 383 6864 ♦ fax: 812 355 4082

By the same author

The Chronicles of a Wanderer
Camping with the Penguins

Introduction

One Woman's Scrapbook is a series of reflections, an intimate collection of writings.

When I was young I thought travelling was for explorers. But one day my sister and I were wandering along one of the lanes that wound its way through our village when we saw a man coming towards us. He stopped and asked the way. He said he was lost. His English was poor and we invited him for tea. Mother, always friendly welcomed him. He said he lived in Switzerland and had been sent to England to learn the language. "Switzerland" he said, "is a beautiful country! Perhaps you will visit us one day."

Years later we had that privilege and I fell in love with the Swiss Alps. That was the beginning of my wanderlust. I have always enjoyed the mountainous terrain and have climbed through Canada's Rocky Mountains. We didn't reach the top, neither did we aspire to such heights, but climbing was spiritually uplifting. Returning to our campsite, we sat around the log-fire and enjoyed our hot rums while the stars looked down upon us. And now, as I read my diaries the memories all come flooding back and my books will be my legacy for my children and grandchildren for years to come.

Preface

I had a good start in life. My parents were happy, both were avid gardeners and both loved dogs. I have fond memories of them walking arm-in-arm around the garden, with the dog scampering along beside them.

We lived in an agricultural village in Kent where the inhabitants were known for their longevity. There was an hourly bus service to towns like Margate, Broadstairs and Canterbury. Broadstairs noted for Dickens and his novels, and Canterbury, where I was confirmed many years ago.

After the war my husband and I and our two children immigrated to Australia. There we travelled extensively from Tasmania in the south, to Melbourne, and Brisbane in Queensland further north. We had two more children, now two sons and two daughters.

When they became young adults and all had left home I had a choice. I could have stayed home, fulfilled my daily responsibilities. And I could have been a good grandmother but I was free, free for the first time ever. I decided to travel.

My elder daughter had immigrated to Canada, she sponsored me. During my first two years in Canada I worked my way from the Pacific to the Atlantic. I met wonderful people, fell in love with Canada and Canadians, and the Rocky Mountains.

I visit Australia every other year, I enjoy my family and watch the progress of my grandchildren, and in the back of my mind there is always the possibility that I might, one day, return.

Table of Contents

A Tribute To My Parents:

February 21 1915 at Thanet House, Sarre, in the small hours of the morning, my mother gave birth to a little girl, and the matter-of-fact midwife exclaimed, "My, what a pretty child!" The infant's head was actually covered with fair curls.

I was baptized shortly afterwards in the local Protestant Church in the village of St. Nicholas and given the names

Joan Mary Packham. Later I was confirmed in Canterbury Cathedral.

I had one sister, Stella Muriel, born in 1912. And one brother, Eric Charles, born 1920.

I lived my first six years of life in Sarre and soon after Eric was born we moved to St. Nicholas. My sister was a sickly child and as Sarre was in a valley, constantly submerged in mist from the low-lying marshlands my parents moved to higher levels.

My father built our home in an orchard surrounded by green pastures. My memories are all peaceful; the areas all agricultural, birds and sheep were my companions when I would wander off alone with the dog.

My earliest recollection was during World War 1. Being carried downstairs to the cellars below as bombs were falling. I don't remember the bombs, only a man in a dark suit and sitting on his knee on a bench behind a red curtain - I don't know who the man was.

That cellar had very happy memories for me. At the bottom of the stairs it branched out in both directions; one side was the coal-cellar and the coalman tipped sacks of coal through the grid in the lane that lead to our garden. Logs and kindling were also kept there. The other side of the cellar had slatted wooden shelves for storing the fruit. I was always an early riser and before breakfast would take my rope to the cellar and skip. My only companions were the little efts(or newts), a type of small lizard that scampered in and out all over the floor.

I know little of my parents except that my father was born and married in St. Nicholas and lived there all his life. His father came from Dymchurch in Kent. My father was one of ten brothers and three sisters and as happened in those days children died young of T.B. or infants and mothers died in childbirth. Only seven survived to adulthood. I don't remember any of my grandparents. My father, Walter Packham, only had one holiday and that was on his honeymoon when he took my mother to Bruges in Belgium.

My mother was a Loft. The Lofts came from Scandinavia in years gone by. My grandfather Loft owned a Public House in Sarre, the Cherry Brandy House dated 1666 and was halfway between London and Dover in the days of stagecoaches. It was there that my parents met and fell in love.

I know little of my mother but I am going to write some of her early experiences as she told them to me. She was christened Minnie, a name she utterly disliked, and so she always signed her name Minna. She, and her two older sisters went to a private school in Twickenham. She was the youngest of eleven children. When she left school she became a telephonist in the days of British rule in India, and she was invited to go there with her company, but her love of her mother prevented her from going. Sadly, her mother died soon afterwards.

I grew up with the guiding hands of my parents. Those formative years set the tone for my adult existence.

I loved them equally but differently and with an unquestioning trust.

For my mother I would gather little nosegays from the hedgerows and carry them home for her and no matter how wilted my offerings, they were always cherished. I loved my mother very dearly and would discuss all my problems with her, the problems that seemed so large then, and I listened to her advice. I know now that she was not always right but I respected her judgement and was devastated when she died. She was only 54.

My father I admired for the kindnesses he showed toward everyone and I never heard him say an unkind word. He was generous and gentle with all who knew him. He went to church regularly and sang in the choir. My mother played the piano and together they taught us all, the joy of singing.

Father was a great storyteller. We would sit round the log fire on dark winter evenings and he told us stories about a little Black Boy who was always into mischief. And sometimes he would talk to us about the smuggling days, quoting Rudyard Kipling's famous Smugglers Song:

> Them that ask no questions
> Isn't told a lie.
> Watch the wall, my darling
> While the gentlemen go by.

Then he told us tales of the rum runners and excise men. My grandparents kept the Sun Inn in our village of St Nicholas where I lived from the age of about seven. The village was on the edge of the marshes that ran down to the North Sea, and flowed into the English Channel separating England from France.

When my father was a boy he remembered lying in bed and listening to the wind howling on dark winter evenings and he knew that ships would land on the coast, and the rum runners would be waiting with their pack horses to collect their booty. The church, he said, was even used as a storehouse. There was a secret underground passage leading to the cellar of the Sun Inn, and the casks of brandy were passed through a small trapdoor in the floor of the bar.

When the excise men, or revenue officers called, word of mouth preceded them, and the rum hidden away in another smaller cellar that was never discovered. And any lace my Grandmother Packham had acquired through smuggling, was wound round-and-around her waist under her crinoline.

The Southeast corner of Kent was infamous for its illicit trafficking, evading the import and export duties. They were known as the smuggling gentlemen, and called themselves free traders.

But my most peaceful recollections are of my parents walking arm-in-arm together through the garden with the little terrier scampering along beside them; wandering over the croquet lawn towards the orchard where the deckchairs awaited them. In the springtime the blossoms would attract the bees and there would be the constant drone as they flew from one flower to another.

In the wintertime we all sat round the log fire before going to bed, mother in one chair, father in another smoking his pipe. Sometimes father would tell us a story, sometimes mother would read to us before we went to our rooms and were tucked into bed for the night.

The Sound Of Music:

*M*usic has influenced my life since the very beginning. Our home was always full of music. My father was a chorister.

Our mother taught us our early lullabies and nursery rhymes as her fingers wandered over the keys, and sometimes, our father sang in harmony with us.

As my sister and I grew older we were sent to a convent near Canterbury. I remember a nun, Sister St. Lelia, a beautiful woman, even in her black habit she looked regal and dignified. She had a rich voice and taught us to sing, carrying us through our scales and arpeggios, psalms and anthems.

I sang in the school choir and took an active part in the end of year school concerts when our parents and friends filled the hall and listened with great pride as we all performed. During our last year we were taken to symphony concerts and taught how to listen and appreciate, and understand when to applaud, and when not to. It was part of the school curriculum.

We grew up in rural England and going to church was a part of village life, and when I was in my teens I was allowed to play the church organ. It was a wonderful feeling. Even the simplest melody swelled the sounds, and raised the roof to the power of welcome. Music is one of the most universal of man's arts. People have expressed emotions in music from earliest time.

It is the same in every country regardless of language. My home is still full of the sound of music but now days I am content with symphonies, concertos and chamber music, all played on tape.

Saved By The Bell:

$\mathcal{G}$ood! What is good?

I have been asked to write about a good deed, something that I have done that was good. Where does one start? I'm not good. I can go to church and look good, but that doesn't make me good. I can be competent and dependable, does that make me good? I can give a helping hand sometimes, that doesn't make me good or does it? Good is like love, something one does, but does not talk about.

Once upon-a-time when I was very small, four years old to be precise, I did something that was good, I suppose. So, I will begin at the beginning.

My story begins in an old Victorian home on the edge of the marshes. There were many rooms in this house. My parents lived there, I was born there in the pink room between the nursery and the blue room.

My sister was two-and-a-half years older than I. We were not a bit alike. Molly was always into trouble of one kind or another and sometimes I wondered why she did it.

I used to like pleasing people. Did that make me good? My sister resented parental discipline and would always do the opposite if she could get away with it. Did that make her bad?

Downstairs were many more rooms; one was the sitting room used on special occasions, and on this particular afternoon my mother was entertaining and we were waiting for the guests to arrive.

I suppose we were bored with ourselves and decided to play at being bears and while we were rollicking around on all fours, Molly bumped into a table sending a beautiful piece of pottery flying and smashing into smithereens. I looked at my sister's woebegone face, picked up the pieces, took them to my mother and confessed my guilt. Whether my mother guessed, or knew, I shall never know, because at that moment I was saved by the bell sounding through the hall announcing the arrival of the guests.

*Excerpts from
my mother's letters
to her brother
in America.
1939—1940*

September 27 1938

Today we have all been fitted with gas masks. Young and old we all went along to the village hall. I can still smell the rubber. They talk of the whole of Thanet being evacuated. Joan is working at the mask depot at Westgate from the time she leaves Doon House until ten o'clock tonight. The school is to be evacuated soon.

It is all a great worry and we can only hope and pray that Hitler will be made to see reason before it is too late. The Prime Minister is broadcasting tonight at eight o'clock. He has been wonderfully plucky to fly over to Hitler on his mission of peace. I heard Hitler's speech to Germany last night, he is a fanatic, we are preparing for the worst.

November 25 1940

$\mathcal{M}$y last letter to you was returned it didn't pass the censor so we will see if this reaches you. We are well despite rations of butter, sugar, tea and meat. But we are fortunate as we have a good vegetable garden and an orchard with all kinds of fruits including apples, plums, nectarines, peaches, and plenty of cherries, gooseberries, rhubarb etc., and we make do with a minimum of sugar. It is one of the advantages of living in the country. City dwellers are having a more difficult time.

Being so near to the coast there is something going on all the time, chiefly raids, and daily dogfights overhead. I have had a few terrifying experiences, but it all happens very suddenly. One afternoon during the summer I was having tea in the summerhouse and sirens and dog fights had been going on more or less all day long, but suddenly shots rattled against the summerhouse and to my horror I saw a Spitfire diving around a Messerschmitt very low down. I flung myself into the corner and grabbed the hood of the mowing machine and put it over my head; but it was all over very quickly and we fetched the German down in the field near us. On another occasion Jerrys had been droning overhead all day long, you get used to it but when I saw a low flying Jerry I flew for my life as it skimmed the roof with a Spitfire after him. He was brought down in flames, a line of black smoke and then the sickening crash. During the day one of our boys was brought down and the Spitfire fell nearby, the airman was flung into a cottage garden and died soon afterwards. Many Germans have been shot down.

When a Dornier was shot down the other morning early, we thought we would go and have a look at it (the risks we take!) and just as we reached it an Army Officer caught sight of us, and we were hastily escorted away from the scene, he said, "Come away quickly, there are four Germans lying all over the place."

Margate and Ramsgate have been heavily bombed with most shops boarded up; it begins to look awful. Eric's last day of leave we decided to go and have a look around Margate and have tea and a Cinema (Fred Astaire). We no sooner arrived at the Clock Tower and were surveying the damage when several Jerrys swooped out of the clouds overhead with our Spitfires after them. Did we run? We were soon in an underground shelter!

Canterbury has been heavily bombed but so far the Cathedral has escaped damage. Although the Deanery received a direct hit and the Dean had a narrow escape sheltering in a passage. But parts of Canterbury were not so lucky and there was a great deal of loss of life and whole streets were demolished.

Sarre, too, the cottages just behind the Cherry Brandy House received a direct hit killing two people but the Cherry Brandy House survived.

Molly is in the Air Force; she joined up soon after the war commenced and is secretary to a Wing Commander. And Eric volunteered for the Air Force and was accepted about six weeks later. He is stationed near Coventry. He returned last Friday morning after his first weeks leave, the morning following the dreadful slaughter of poor Coventry. When he left here we had no idea it was

Coventry that got it so badly, we just heard the broadcast; "A Midlandtown." I have waited ten days for his letter telling of his experiences . This is an extract:

"I managed to get back to camp, but what a journey! After leaving home at 10 a.m. I arrived at Victoria Station at 12.30, and made my way to Euston, only to find there were no trains for Coventry. I was sent to St. Pancras and caught a special train to Leicester. After an hours run we came to Bedford, so I thought I would get out there and catch a train to Northampton. I arrived here at 6:30 just as the sirens went. Anyway nothing happened and the next stop was Rugby. Again I had to change trains and the nearest I could get to Coventry was Leamington, nine miles away, so on I jumped. It was a slow journey, the train stopped constantly and it was 9 pm by this time. I made a few enquiries here re Coventry only to find nobody was allowed near there. So I went to the Police Station and asked what they could do about it. After a few ums and ahs it was decided that they could spare a special policeman to run me back by car, or anyway as far as they were allowed to go. We were stopped two miles out of Leamington. So the driver told them that he had an R.A.F. Officer in the back of the car who had to get back that night. It worked, and I arrived just as the Ack Ack guns opened fire at 10 p.m.

The next day:

I went to Coventry this afternoon and have not long been back. We had to walk both ways because what buses were available were being used to get the homeless out into the country. It was a pitiful sight. Coventry itself is wicked. There is nothing left standing in the shopping centre and fires are still burning. The Cathedral is just a heap of bricks, stone and mortar with just the four walls left standing and the towering spire. They are still searching for bodies in the ruins of the Cathedral; people who were sheltering in the vaults before the blitz started. Two or three land mines were dropped and today we saw one lying in the side of a byroad. Unfortunately there is a delayed action bomb very near so when that goes off the mine is bound to explode. One land mine dropped outside Coventry, and the nose of it is now being used as a washtub. There is no gas, electricity and in many cases no water and it is impossible to buy anything at all.

The king came to see us today. We saw his car but were unable to wait to see him."

Joan has had two skirmishes but she seems to take it all in stride:

The first time a bomb fell nearby and the blast blew her across the road and into a doorway. The door slammed on her hand. She couldn't get up and some soldiers rescued her. Her thumbnail was ripped in half and the bone in her thumb was fractured.

The second time she was driving the car having delivered some groceries to the shepherd who lives out on the marsh, when she saw a Messerschmitt coming towards her. She rammed on the brakes, threw herself out of the car and into the gutter as the side window was sprayed with bullets.

As I write, windows and doors are shaking, they have been rattling all day long shelling to and from Dover. The remarkable thing is we have become used to it, just as we have become accustomed to the wailing of the sirens. We pray that it will soon end.

Minna.

The Winter Of Discontent:

*T*he winter of 1940 was one of the worst ever recorded. The roads were buried beneath drifting snow as the first conveys were driven towards their Army Barracks when everything came to a standstill. One of the lorries had skidded and turned over blocking everything in its path.

It was a terrible year.

The soldiers were cold, dispirited and unhappy. It was December. They were all missing their families, homes and loved ones. They carried with them tea and cocoa, and came to us for hot water.

We were told there was a young solder who was ill. An Officer came to the door. He was young and looked as unhappy as all the rest. He asked if they could bring the young man into the shelter of our home and my mother said, "Yes, of course!" We hastily made up a bed on the floor in front of the fire and they brought him in and placed him there.

While mother warmed some chicken broth I stayed with him. I put my hand on his forehead, it was hot and I whispered to him, "I know you will get well." He opened his eyes and smiled, I knew he understood although he was too weak to speak. Mother supported him while he sipped some of the broth. He was only nineteen years old. Eventually the Royal Army Medical Corps took him away on a stretcher. He died of pneumonia a few days later.

A Night To Remember:

$\mathcal{I}$t was a glorious moonlight night. I was a Warden waiting to go on night duty when the sirens wailed as the Luftwaffe flew over the English Channel on its way to London attacking British coastal airfields and ports.

My father was in bed when there was an enormous explosion, a doodlebug had fallen nearby. Everything seemed to fall in around us. I picked my way through the rubble to my father who was lying there looking up into the stars. "Phew," he said, "That was close!"

"Why aren't you in the shelter?" I asked.

"If I am going to be bombed, I am going to be bombed in comfort," was his reply.

Once we had recovered from the shock we picked our way through the total chaos to the kitchen to make a cup of tea. In emergencies like that it was the odd **cuppa** that saved the sanity of the Brits during the war. But there was a blackout, no electricity, no gas! However, we had a hay box made from a plywood tea chest. Every evening before going to bed when there was electricity we filled a large pot with boiling water and immersed it in the hay. It stayed hot for many hours and we were able to have our cup of tea.

There was no more sleep that night as the bombers flew over in waves and attacked London. My brother was with Bomber Command, flying sorties night after night, and was never far from our thoughts.

Suddenly my father said, "Where's the dog?" Daniel was a terrier and a little treasure. He didn't come when we called and there was nothing we could do until the All Clear sounded. When it was light enough to see we went outside. "Danny!" we called. We thought we heard a whimper. We listened, and called again, then we heard him. We followed the sound and found one frightened little dog trapped beneath some bricks when the corner of our home collapsed. We pulled him out and spoke comforting and soothing words and stroked his quivering little body and held him tight. I wrapped him in a blanket and gave him to my father. Grabbing my gas mask and tin hat I rushed through the village to the church and climbed the stairs to the top of the tower and joined two other Wardens. With binoculars focussed across the English Channel to the French coast we watched - and waited for the invasion that we all feared and expected.

Kent became a battleground and the sirens became a familiar sound. Aerodromes, shipping and the coastal towns were attacked. Dover, only a few minutes flying time from our village was heavily bombed. We watched for any sign of movement and in the event of invasion we would have rung the church bells warning people to take cover. Mercifully that did not happen and we only learned, long afterwards, that Hitler commanded that Dover Castle be spared; that was where he planned his first meal when he set foot on English soil.

Bequet's Story:

$\mathcal{I}$ am a Channel Islander. I grew up in Jersey and spent my early childhood there before being sent away to boarding school in England, and then France. My mother and father had a large home near St. Brelarde's Bay, and my father taught me the art of sailing.

I had a very happy young life and loved the water, and I don't know why I did not join the Navy when war broke out. Instead, I joined the Army and was sent to England, where I met my dream girl.

I used to think about the Channel Islands. They were largely self-governing and not bound by any Acts of Parliament, although they were a part of Britain. We owned a property and kept cattle, Jersey and Guernsey cows mostly, and everything was peaceful and harmonious until the German forces occupied the islands, and I never saw, or heard, from my family again.

In England, I was stationed with my unit in a little village on the Kent coast, prior to being sent overseas. It was a Godforsaken place really. All the women and children had been sent away, leaving a sprinkling of people to work the land and run the businesses, church and pubs.

The troops spent time in the pubs. There they found warmth and comfort and after a drink or two, they forgot their woes and sang Roll Out The Barrel, and There'll always be an England, and several rather more scurrilous ditties, and at closing time the singing continued all the way back to their billets. Each day there were route marches and training for what was yet to come. There were continuous dogfights by day and raids by night when our guns opened fire and the noise echoed and reverberated through the hills.

I was enjoying a watered-down beer in the Bell Inn, a quaint old pub, with low ceilings and dark oak panelling, when three girls walked in. We invited them to join us. There were ten of us and only three girls. It was Stephanie I liked and suggested we walk together to escape the noise in the bar. We had not gone far when the sirens wailed and we all rushed back to camp leaving the girls to fend for themselves, but we did agree to meet the following day.

I grew to like my dream girl and fantasized about settling down in my beloved Jersey, and hoped the farm would still be there when the war ended.

Then rumours started to circulate, and talk of being sent across the English Channel was on everyones mind. The route marches intensified and the time came for us to pack up, and move on. I took my girl for our last walk and we promised to love each other always and to write often. We kept that promise, it was her letters that gave me hope.

Then came the final leave. She was standing by the gate waiting. We rushed into each other's arms and my girl wept with joy. It was the happiest forty-eight hours of my life. We were united; we were one. Then it was time to leave. We were overcome by a sense of finality that so many others were feeling but never voicing. Would_ we ever see each other again? It was a question we asked ourselves, but never asked each other.

We crowded into the boat, so tightly packed we could scarcely move. As we neared the French coast the barrage of shells was horrendous. We dropped over the edge of the carrier into the water and scrambled, soaking wet, along the shore. It was a wild and! chilling night, so dark we had no idea where we were or where we were going, but I found myself beside a fellow officer and nearby was a cottage, barely discernible against the trees. They had a small holding and took us in. They gave us food and shelter for the night.

These wonderful people were working 'underground'. They risked their lives to save ours.

* * * * * * * * * * * * * * * * * * * *

That was the last Stephanie heard from Bequet. Weeks passed before she received news of Bequet's death. He had been shot and killed by a snipers bullet. Stephanie kept Bequet's letters and cherished them. Even though she knew them by heart, she read them over and over again.

Time Was Of The Essence:

We met in 1942. One of the wealthy farmers in the village gave a 21st birthday party for his son. They had hired the village hall and because it was wartime all the young men had been called up. There were quite a number of young women, their numbers swelled by the Land Army billeted there. I, and two friends went together. The hall was almost devoid of men. We knew the Officers from the Mess had been invited so we decided to go to the nearby pub and rout them out.

That was the beginning of my emancipation. Until the war, young ladies did not visit such public places unaccompanied. The few locals seemed surprised when they saw us enter, but disregarding them we approached a bunch of khaki-clad Officers. They were bored and delighted to see us. Soon the watered-down beer was flowing and it didn't take long for us to persuade them to join the party.

My husband-to-be monopolised me, and I wished he wouldn't, as I had my eye on another fellow. When it was all over John escorted me home. I invited him in for a drink and to my surprise he sat down to the piano and played. I was soon to learn that he could play anything by ear.

Three weeks later we were married in a Registrar's Office in London. Our night was disrupted by sirens and bombs. Several times we had to get up and flee to the shelters until the All Clear sounded. What a night it was! At the same time it was exciting and rather fun. Those of us, the more intrepid ones, went up on the roof to watch the incendiary bombs falling and London burning. I'll never forget it. The courtship was short and my husband of a few hours was soon on his way to Yorkshire to join the convoy, which would take him and his Regiment to Europe.

A Narrative:

*M*y husband grew up in London. His mother was an Austrian, and his father came from Germany, Holzer by name. His father was in a prisoner- of- war camp where he remained for the duration of the war. He was a dear gentle man and a professional artist. He said, "It was my art that saved my sanity."

When my husband left university he studied medicine in London and changed his name by Deed Poll. He said, "With a name like Holzer I would have no practice," and he changed his name to Woodley, and joined the Army. He was billeted in St. Nicholas before being sent to Europe. He played the violin and together we had many happy hours playing duets.

When he was demobilized he returned to his hospital in London and studied anaesthesiology. It was there that he met an Australian surgeon who persuaded my husband to immigrate to Australia. He said, "It is a wonderful country in which to bring up a family." With the passage of time John became disenchanted with orthodox medicine and when he had his sabbatical leave he went to Hong Kong, London and Paris and studied acupuncture. On his return I was his guinea pig. I had suffered from sciatica for months. Five treatments and I was completely cured. John opened a clinic in one of Melbourne's hospitals, and a private clinic from home. Business was brisk and the hospital overflowing with people who were tired of taking pills for pain. This was his rewarding legacy.

John died peacefully in his sleep at the age of eighty-six.

Life Begins At 65:

$\mathcal{B}$ efore my Uncle Sydney retired, he used to go off to Whitehall in the city, wearing his dark suit and bowler hat, and carrying his rolled umbrella.

He would reminisce and talk to us about his life and plans for the future. And this is what he told us:

"For years his life had been the same until the dreariness of his routine no longer seemed to matter. There was always the annual holiday to look forward to, usually hiking through the Western Counties of England. He married late and was widowed early but in his wife's lifetime they would bed-and-breakfast their way through Dorset, Devon and Cornwall. When he eventually retired he was given a gold watch and chain, and jokingly told us how surprised he was to find the presentation meant little to him after all his years of service."

Once my uncle became accustomed to reading the morning paper over a leisurely breakfast he began to think about putting his plans and dreams into action. Eve though he was alone he wanted to buy a cottage in the country, and to have a dog for companionship, then the two of them could wander off together through the bracken and the heather, and scramble over the hills and moorlands.

Sydney was fascinated with the Cornish coast and told us tales that the fisher folk had told him. Tales of storms and shipwrecks, and French invasions of long ago. So one bright sunny morning he took the train to Penzance and hired a car.

It was wonderful country to explore, and rounding a bend in a lane off the beaten track, Sydney came upon a little broken down dwelling. It had been for sale for a long time by the look of it, everything was overgrown with blackberries, the sign almost obliterated. Sydney felt he was trespassing as he made his way through the undergrowth to the cottage and peeped through the windows. The cottage was build of stone and its main attraction was its dormer windows set into the sloping thatched roof. My uncle was delighted. There were so many possibilities he could hardly contain his excitement.

The garden was untamed but it was on the top of the cliffs overlooking the water that so stimulated his imagination. Sydney visualized the time when he would grow all his own fruit and vegetables. He was completely captivated!

My uncle hurried to the Real Estate Agent in Penzance and without further ado, signed the Agreement and the transaction was completed. The following weeks were fraught with anxiety and apprehension as he put his town house on the market. He said he simply couldn't sleep! But he need not have worried, the house sold and with the formalities behind him the day eventually dawned when he set off for Cornwall to commence his new life.

Sydney bought a little black and white puppy that followed him everywhere, a pert game little dog, named Fellow. My uncle found a village lad to help him, and together they worked repairing the cottage and tilling the soil until the garden was cultivated. Sydney watched his vegetables grow with pride and interest and when he was able to gather them he said they were better than anything he had ever bought in the shops.

Sydney was a tall fair man of Scandinavian descent and his eyes were as blue as the water on a clear sunny day, becoming bluer as he grew older. And as the years passed, his toil in the rain, wind and sunshine gave him a weathered look.

I used to love to go and stay with him. He was my favourite uncle and I treasured our times together. He transformed the ramshackle cottage into a charming home. He raised the roof and added more rooms, but the living room we loved most of all; it was intimate and filled with memories. The walls were lined with books and in the winter months there was always a log fire blazing in the grate.

Sydney was a remarkable man. He talked to us about many things and how times had changed in the past, almost one hundred years. He was active in three wars. As a young man he had fought in the Boer War. During World War 1, he had survived the trenches of Flanders and Paschendaele. And in World War 11 he had joined the Civil Defence, and watched his home crumble into a heap of rubble when a V2 missile fell nearby.

Sydney was quite content to live alone. I asked him if he was ever lonely and his reply was, "How could I be with all this? I'm blessed! I have my home with a view in all its changing moods, I have my books, my music, and my Fellow," he said, giving an affectionate pat to the dog. "What more could I possibly want?"

One day I asked my uncle to what he attributed his longevity and he said, "growing my own vegetables," and when he was seventy he said he felt himself getting younger and younger. Possibly, he might have lived to be one hundred years old had he not slipped in his garden in the rain and lost consciousness. My Uncle Sydney was taken to the hospital in Penzance where he died of pneumonia. He was ninety-six.

Brizes Park:

E veryone said, "You won't get a job." "Why not," I thought. Admittedly my hair was white and I was nearly sixty, but I had been white since I was thirty. I scanned the LONDON TIMES and the DAILY TELEGRAPH. There were heaps of jobs for nannies and housekeepers, and an agency that promised to Solve Your Problem.

Taking the underground to Kensington I found the agency and with much aplomb walked in. A friendly woman greeted me and asked if she could help. "Yes," I said, "I need a short term job." She picked five cards from her file. I had a choice. I chose the one I thought I would be able to do.

The interview took place in Kensington Palace Gardens, off Bayswater Road in London, where many ambassadors to the Court of St. James have their residences. While we drank tea from fine bone china, Lady Sylvia DeBellaigue told me about her uncle who needed someone to care for him while his companion/nurse was in hospital recovering from the shingles.

The following day we drove to Brizes Park, in Essex. It was a mansion! The uncle was a tall handsome man in his late seventies. He lived alone with his dog in three hundred acres of woodlands, cornfields and green pastures. At the entrance was the Lodge.

On arrival it was as though I had stepped back in time. I was introduced to all the staff. Each member had his own roll to play from those who cleaned the brass and copper, to the chauffeur, and the gardener who supplied the vegetables. When the day ended the staff returned to the village and there were just the two of us. Before leaving, the odd-job man offered to lock-up and close the windows. I asked him to show me the routine as it was June and the evenings were long so it seemed a pity to close out the sunshine and the daylight hours. The windows and the shutters were immense and a heavy iron rod had to be swung across to secure them.

I was shown over the house from the kitchen to the butler's pantry and through the many rooms including the Honourable Simon Rodney's study, where he spent most of his time when he was not on the estate. The study was the most interesting room of them all. Simon had a collection of paintings adorning the walls, some of Admiral Rodney, the same Admiral who became famous for his naval battles in the 18th century. Simon told me that he was a direct descendant of the Admiral. Another collectors' item was a blue velvet chair that had belonged to Queen Elizabeth at the time of her Coronation. He was also Winston Churchill's cousin.

A blue carpet covered the wide staircase that led from the centre of the flagstone hall to a semi-circular balcony with suites leading from it. Mine was at the opposite end of the gallery to Simon Rodney's. I had a rose coloured carpet, some books, a desk, fireplace, and a huge four-poster bed. The view from the window looked across the estate in the front, over a sea of golden cornfields and green pastures, with a few Fresian black and white cows dotted about. It was supremely peaceful. At the back, my suite overlooked the cobbled courtyard and stables. Only one horse remained, a chestnut stallion that Simon named Simple.

Once the staff had left for the day everything seemed quiet and strange, as it always does in unfamiliar places. I wandered to the kitchen, there was an Aga cooker; I remembered my mother cooking with one many years ago and how delicious were her rock buns and scones and hoped mine would be as good. The floor was of flagstone and there was a large Deal table in the centre of the room. The brasses on the walls shone from years of polish, reflecting images, making the space around bright and light.

After dinner Simon Rodney showed me the estate. We took Peter, the dog, on our walk. There was a walled garden for vegetables and fruit trees of all kinds. The paths were lined with herbaceous beds, roses and sweet peas filled the night air with perfume. Simon's pride was his greenhouse collection of orchids and other exotic plants, which we watered together before wandering home when Simon decided to go to his room. I went with him, turned down his bed covers and left him with his book.

Taking Peter again, I walked all around the building as I wanted to know how many exits there were, and to make sure all the doors were locked and the windows secured. I followed the dog to a field that lead to a creek. It was a glorious evening and the moon cast long shadows over the property making the world around us appear **ethereal**. I thought how fortunate I was to be living in such beautiful surroundings and being paid for the privilege of being there.

On our return I again peeped at Simon Rodney to make sure everything was well with him. The dog put himself to bed on the stairs under the chandelier that was left burning all night like a beacon.

After a while I, too, went to my room. Climbing into bed I had visions of the people who might have lived there, the type of life they would have lived, the balls, the gowns and the hunting parties. For some reason an unease began to creep over me, and a chill, that was quite unreasonable and unexplainable. I tried to sleep and must have dozed because I woke with a start when there was a loud thump. I sat bolt upright and listened; had I dreamed it? And what of the man I was supposed to be looking after? I knew nothing of him. I heard sounds, and in my subconscious mind recalled the hollow ring of loose flagstones as I was being shown through the hall. Getting off my bed as quietly as possible I crept to the window. In the silence, everything seemed to creak. I didn't know what I expected to see and in the moonlight could see nothing and no one. Then a door slammed! I shot with the speed of terror into Simon Rodney's room only to find him fast asleep. I shook him saying "there is someone in the house." He looked at me as though I may be a little touched (he told me later) and said "you stay here." But I wouldn't, and together we went down the staircase that passed the dining room. The door, which I knew I had closed, was open. "My God," he exclaimed "we've been burgled!" The drawer from the sideboard was missing together with the entire silver cutlery. "Call the police," Simon shouted. I dashed to the nearest telephone and dialled 999. Without further thought I grabbed Peter and we ran around the house and through the gardens following footmarks imprinted in the dewy grass, which lead straight to the creek, and there we lost them. Thwarted, we returned home.

Simon was sitting in his study and beginning to show signs of shock. As I could not find his robe, and he didn't know where it was, I wrapped him in a blanket and gave him a strong whiskey. We waited in the study until the police arrived with tracker dogs. They scoured the

grounds, but found nothing other than the footprints. They concluded that the thieves with their spoil had walked along the creek-bed to a waiting car on the road, and they would already be on their way across the English Channel to France, where it would all be sold. The policemen left saying they would return in the morning.'

I took Simon back to his room and tucked him into bed before returning to my room, but sleep eluded me. To pass the time I went down to the kitchen to make some tea and was shocked to find a man there; it was the Lodge gatekeeper. "Did they take much?" he asked. "How did you know?" I retorted. He turned deathly white, then flushed and left abruptly. When he had gone I made sure the door was locked from the inside and the bolt securely drawn. But it unnerved me and I wished the night would end.

When the police returned Simon, took them through the house to see what was missing. (When they left previously, we had been warned to touch nothing.) The study remained undisturbed.

Across the hall, opposite the study, was the drawing room, completely ransacked and stripped of all its antiques and valuable silver pieces. Evidentially, they took the drawer from the dining room, through the drawing room, throwing into it everything they could quickly gather and left through the double doors at the far end of the room leading to the garden. Nothing was ever recovered.

The mystery remained as to who had done it. My belief was that someone knew the house and the area. The dog had not barked. Why? My mind went back to the man in the kitchen. Later, I learned he had been dismissed and although I don't believe he did it, I think he knew who did.

Their means of entry was at the rear of the house. A low oblong window ran parallel with a passage. The bar

across the window was a long heavy wooden beam and with years of wear and tear it had worn away. With the aid of a crowbar they broke the window and moved the bar from side to side until it was loose enough to be lifted and thrown to the floor. That was the thump that initially woke me.

Following the stresses of my first night at Brizes Park, life settled down to a more conventional symmetry. Simon and I became good friends. We walked many miles together, either on the estate or through the country lanes that bounded his property. Occasionally, the chauffeur drove us and we looked at old churches, and pubs where we stopped for a pint of the best draught beer and chatted with the locals. In the evenings we would play cribbage and many a time Simon liked me to read to him. He relished the peace that came with nightfall and sitting around the fire before retiring. Simon was a typical English gentleman with his smoking jacket, slippers and pipe, and Peter always somewhere in the offing.

I enjoyed my six weeks at Brizes Park. It provided me with a unique and unforgettable experience. It also confounded my critics.

Things That Go
Bump In The Night

We had been sitting around that Hallowe'en night, telling stories of ghosts, dreams and other strange experiences, when my mind slipped into the past, and I remembered my uncle's bakery in England, with its shop and thatched roof, and the wonderful, delicious aroma of freshly baked bread.

Behind the store were cobbled stones and stables for the horse, and the sweet, seductive smell of hay. I can still feel the horse's warm breath on my face as I stroked his lovely head and looked into his trusting eyes. Above the stables were lofts, reached only by scrambling up a wooden ladder, and this is where we used to hide with the village kids, and tell stories that grew more exciting and horrific each time the same story was told.

Molly, my sister, two years older than I, was a great storyteller, and used to tell of a dream that never failed to make our blood curdle and send cold shivers down our spines!

"Molly was walking with three young boys, who seemed to be about eight years old. It was flat marshland and one of the boys disappeared. In the distance was a small church. As they drew near, one of the boys suggested the missing boy might be inside. There was a low oblong window, blackened around the edge and it appeared to be on fire. Their footsteps quickened, and beside the door on a nail, hanging by its laces was a small pair of black boots. Molly put her hand inside and felt them to be warm, so she knew they had only recently been worn. She was filled with apprehension as she hurried inside. There were wooden pews and the church was empty, except for a man wearing a black cloak bending over a furnace; he was stuffing something into the red-hot embers and two small legs were dangling outside.

Molly was beside herself with rage and fury. On the pew near the furnace was a cardboard box filled with garden tools. She grabbed a small fork; she wanted to kill him! At the same time, he took a bottle of clear fluid, pulled the cork, and started sprinkling it over her. She knew it was lethal and he was going to set light to her when she awoke shouting and screaming for help!"

We scrambled down the ladder leaving the past behind, and found ourselves once again in the present. By this time, we were all convinced it was not a dream at all, and that ghoulies and ghosties really do exist, together with long legged beasties, and things that go bump in the night.

Echoes From The Past:
by Joan Woodley

*W*e left Canada May 29 1990 and flew to Heathrow arriving the next day. Heathrow was enormous but clearly directed and we found the bus that took us to Victoria Station and the Grosvenor Hotel, a delightful old world place modernized with chintzes and chandeliers, altogether a joy and a quiet haven despite the close proximity to Victoria Station in the heart of London.

A porter took us to our room on the 4th floor; it was smoke-proofed and security-proofed. My daughter and I tossed our bags on to our beds and went in search of a restaurant and a light meal before relaxing in a hot bath and tumbling into bed.

We had barely dozed off when the fire alarm sounded. We scrambled out of bed, threw on our robes and slippers and joined the silent stream of people moving down the stairs. It reminded me of my sister and I when staying at the Regent Palace in London during the war and the sirens, when we all traipsed downstairs and into the cellars below until the 'all-clear' sounded. So in the midst of the fire alarm ringing all these people, women in partly clad night attire, devoid of all make-up, made a motley mob and an orderly one. We gathered in the lobby below, half doped with sleep until we were told everything was under control.

There was little sleep that night as we were leaving for Canterbury. We caught the 12:29 train, the weather was perfect, almost 80 degrees and there had been no rain for seven weeks.

* * * * * * * * * * * * * * * * * * *

We found a taxi and the driver took us to the Canterbury Gate Hotel, a quaint, interesting building with small rooms but not especially clean. We had to drag our cases up a winding staircase and walk along a boardwalk to our room, which was up among the rooftops of 16th century buildings overlooking the Cathedral. We spent the day wandering around the city, the Cathedral and The King's School, a college for both girls and boys. The streets and lanes were narrower than I remembered with fascinating little shops and coffee places. It was so hot I bought a sun hat.

* * * * * * * * * * * * * * * * * * *

June 1 1990

We packed our bags, paid our account and called a taxi. When it arrived we asked the driver to take us to a good hotel. He drove us to The Victoria. It was only 15 minutes walking distance from the city centre. Our room was spotlessly clean with a splendid bathroom.

Once ensconced we walked back to the city and enjoyed brunch at the County Hotel, a lovely old building.

We then joined a guided tour of the city and the Cathedral. Canterbury is the cradle of English Christianity. The Cathedral became the place of pilgrimage after the murder of Thomas-a-Becket in 1170 and Chaucer immortalised it in his "Canterbury Tales." It contains the tombs of Henry IV, and Edward, the Black Prince.

While some renovations were being made an old painting was discovered hidden away in one of the walls. It had been pain-stakingly cleaned and all the figures were of the softest hues. I enquired as to its age but no one knew, neither did they know the name of the artist.

It was a glorious evening, the sun was setting as we wandered back to our hotel. After a drink in the lounge we had dinner of the most delicious roast pheasant.

* * * * * * * * * * * * * * * * * * *

June 2 1990

Another gorgeous morning! We awoke to the songs of the blackbirds and song thrushes.

We caught the bus to St. Nicholas, passing my old school that looked just as it always had. I didn't recognise my home of long ago with roads widened reducing a large portion of the garden. Where the tennis court had been there was now a house, and the kitchen garden, another home.

The village bore a look of prosperity. All the old flint-stone cottages had been bought by business people who commute daily to the surrounding towns.

We walked down the lane to the farmhouse where Colonel and Mrs Tapp used to live. Mrs Tapp, now in her 80's remembered me briefly before becoming a little confused. When I was 19 I used to teach Robert, their first-born, as he had a T.B. problem and was unable to go to school for a year; Mary 6 and Rodney just 2. In the mornings I taught Robert and after lunch I used to lift him into a long wicker pram, put the baby at the opposite end, and Mary on. her tricycle. Together with the collie dog we walked the lanes while I invented topical stories incorporating the hedgerows, insects and animals as we went along. It was a never ending serial.

Richard, their 4th child lives there now with his four children. He took us down into the monks chapel under the house. We were each given a candle to light the way, as the steps had been cut into the chalk and were uneven. It was a cruciform shaped chapel, with no windows but containing niches in the walls for holding religious vessels. It is thought that another doorway, now blocked,

led into a subterranean passage leading to the church. This hideaway was thought to have been used during the Reformation, the great religious movement of the 1500s.

June 3 1990

We took photographs of the Old Roman Wall and many other interesting buildings from the top of a double -decker bus and it began to rain. We took refuge in the Heritage Museum, dating back to the 400s, from the earliest beginnings of the arrival of the Picts and Scots; the whole history and artifacts, far too much to describe here, through to the present.

During World War 11 Canterbury was heavily bombed. On the night of June 1st 1942, 500 buildings were destroyed and the best part of 3000 damaged with no loss of life. We were told that a band of men kept vigilance all night on the roof of the Cathedral and as fast as the incendiary bombs fell they were extinguished. The Cathedral remained intact surviving both world wars.

We went to the evening service where Molly and I were confirmed ,

July 26 1930. I felt my sister's presence even though she had long since passed on.

THE CANTERBURY CROSS

The original, probably made in the 8th century, was found beneath a street in Canterbury. A replica is mounted on the wall at the west end of the south aisle of the Cathedral nave. Similar replicas, mounted on fragments of Canterbury Cathedral stone, are placed in our Cathedrals in all parts of the world linking them with Canterbury, the Mother Church of the Anglican Communion.

Our brief visit brought back many memories of peace and war. I have explored many lands and written of many places but "There will always be an England where there's a country lane." History doesn't change, the pubs and cathedrals will remain for generations to come, and now it is time for us to move on, there is still much to see before we fly back to Canada.

Computer Magic:

$\mathcal{I}$t was 1938 when I went to stay with a family in Paris. There were three young men, all of military age and Babette, a sophisticated and attractive young woman of sixteen. It was my job to be with Babette and to speak English. Her father was a parliamentarian, a very worried man who feared war was unavoidable. It was bitterly cold that winter but Babette and I used to wrap up in our overcoats and boots and walk along the banks of the River Seine. I learned to eat snails and became accustomed to garlic, and wine with every meal. Christmas Day we were invited to the home of relatives. We sat round the log fire and talked. The food was sumptuous, the coloured lights and Christmas decorations gay. But it was-overshadowed by the conversation which inevitably turned to thoughts of war that was uppermost in everyone's mind.

New Year's Eve Madame de la Crochais was gay and excited. "We mustn't let Hitler spoil the evening, must we?" she said. Monsieur shook his head sadly. The furniture was removed from the hall, the rugs rolled up and taken away and the floor polished until it shone. A quartet was hired and the evening electrified with gaiety. There were many young people there and we danced the evening away. At midnight we all toasted each other with champagne, and when the church bells rang to welcome in the New

Year, Monsieur wept as he said, "Vive la France!" None of us could have imagined that nine months later Britain and France would be at war with Germany. Babette and I corresponded until France was overrun by the Germans without any opposition and I never heard again. I often wondered what became of them.

* * * * * * * * * * * * * * * * * * * *

Sixty-four long years later 2002, I received an e-mail from Briot de la Crochais, one of Babette's nephew's, asking me to get in touch with his aunt. The nephew had found that story on the Internet after my book, The Chronicles of a Wanderer, was published. They all went underground, and they all survived. Now Babette and I correspond all over again.

AUSTRALIA

The Top Of The Mountain

$\mathcal{M}$ ay 1975 1 went to a Health Spa in a mountain resort near Melbourne. The changing foliage was colourful and every bit as vivid as the fall is in Canada.

We had little time for soliloquy until it was all over. From the moment of arrival I was medically examined, put on a treadmill and told 'I would do'. Do what I wondered? Our routine was strenuous from the beginning. Two miles brisk walking each day before breakfast, exercises, swimming, lectures followed by an afternoon siesta of thirty minutes.

Then the climbing began starting with Mt. Tugwell at 2,000 feet and ending with Mt. Donna Buang at 4,000 feet a few days later. No great feat really but the sense of power it gives you to reach the top, toss off your haversack and fling yourself down on the top of the mountain, to feel on top of the world and shout for all to hear, "I've done it," and then to hear the echo reverberating all around you. It is a terrific sense of achievement and a feeling of great power to know that you have done something that you would never have dreamed was possible.

Twelve commenced the climb, but only two reached the top.

And The Rains Came:

We had been in Australia only a short time and were renting a house. We wanted to buy a home. We found a Real Estate agent who showed us what was available but nothing appealed to us until one day, George our realtor rang and said he had "the very thing."

We drove north from Sydney until we came to a turning off the main road. We drove through double white painted gates along an avenue of blue jacarandas and pink oleandas, until we came to the house. Our immediate reaction was one of disappointment; it was tall, square, ugly, with a conical structure on the roof for decoration. But as we walked through the rooms that were large and lofty and saw the view, we warmed towards it. The view overlooked the river meandering through the trees.

Before committing ourselves we found an architect. Our thoughts ran wild. We could remove the top floor totally and attach it to the ground floor and build a veranda all round the outside. We could insulate it to keep it cool and as most tropical homes were built of timber, the possibilities were innumerable, or so we thought. The architect said,

"You can't do that, it would destroy the character of the old historic home!"

Then we met a Dane and his wife at a New Year's Party. Carl was an architect. We took him to see the building we were contemplating buying and what our plans were. He thought it a wonderful idea and visualized it just as we did. We left everything in his capable hands and the end result amazed even us! The central room, the hall, was circular. A staircase led to the conical structure that had been removed from the original building, making a glassed-in viewpoint. It was our dream come true. There was the river, dolphins and pelicans, even koalas up in the trees in the National Park surrounding the area. All the rooms opened off the hall and each room had a door leading on to the veranda, so there was always a through breeze, and every room had a view.

There were no near neighbours. The eucalyptus trees gave us shelter from the sun and were the nesting place for the magpies, and how they sang from dawn until dusk. It was a wonderful family home.

But Australia is a harsh and exciting country with dramatic climatic changes causing bushfires, drought and floods and after years of drought the rains came. We watched as the river, once so calm and peaceful swept everything away in the swirling, rushing torrents. With the children crammed into the car, we took the animals and fled.

When we returned to our dream home to assess the damage we found the river had reached the foot of the steps leading to our veranda before receding. At the height of the cyclone the floodwaters had risen to unpresidented heights and left a trail of destruction in its wake. Buses, travellers stranded, homes flooded, pineapple, ginseng and banana plantations ruined.

But that day, the sun shone, the magpies returned and so did we.

Australian Wildlife

𝒯he koala is possibly the most lovable fur-bearing animal in the world. It is a marsupial, carrying its young in a pouch for about six months, and then it clings to its mothers back. The koala lives almost exclusively on the young leaves of a few species of eucalyptus.

Only once was I fortunate enough to see a duck-billed platypus in the wild and at the time we were living in Tasmania. They are solitary animals and this little platypus came out of a hole in the bank in front of where I was sitting and swam into the stream. They are rare egg-laying, aquatic, furry mammals with webbed feet, a large square bill and a tail, that he uses as a rudder.

Sherbrook Forest is the place for lyrebirds. The male bird displays his lyre-shaped tail, similar to the way a peacock displays his fan. The lyrebird mimics every bird in the forest, and no song could be sweeter. It laughs like a kookaburra, rings as a bellbird rings and embellishes it all with its own sweet melody.

Australia is a vibrant wildlife country. The joyous song of the colourful birds and the constant cooing of the doves is an ever-present song of happiness.

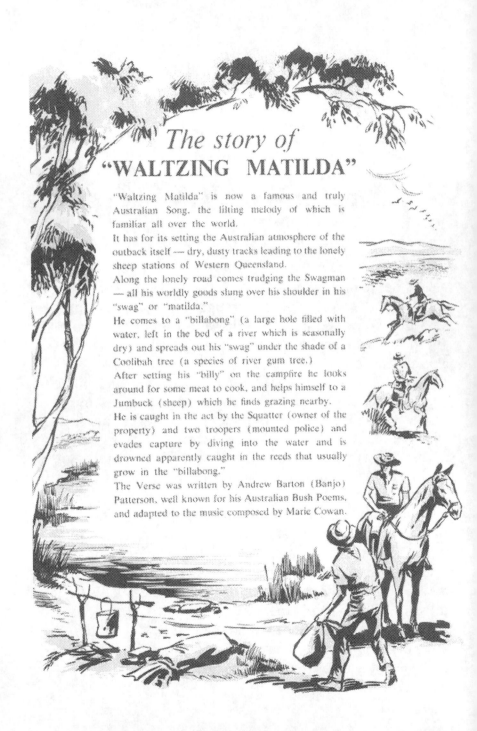

The story of
"WALTZING MATILDA"

"Waltzing Matilda" is now a famous and truly Australian Song, the lilting melody of which is familiar all over the world.

It has for its setting the Australian atmosphere of the outback itself — dry, dusty tracks leading to the lonely sheep stations of Western Queensland.

Along the lonely road comes trudging the Swagman — all his worldly goods slung over his shoulder in his "swag" or "matilda."

He comes to a "billabong" (a large hole filled with water, left in the bed of a river which is seasonally dry) and spreads out his "swag" under the shade of a Coolibah tree (a species of river gum tree.)

After setting his "billy" on the campfire he looks around for some meat to cook, and helps himself to a Jumbuck (sheep) which he finds grazing nearby.

He is caught in the act by the Squatter (owner of the property) and two troopers (mounted police) and evades capture by diving into the water and is drowned apparently caught in the reeds that usually grow in the "billabong."

The Verse was written by Andrew Barton (Banjo) Patterson, well known for his Australian Bush Poems, and adapted to the music composed by Marie Cowan.

Tasmanian Misadventure:
by Joan Woodley

I came around the corner and saw her leaning against the wail looking as white as a ghost. What could have happened?

Six days earlier four of us had set out to hike our way through Cradle Mountain, in the Lake St. Clair National Park in Tasmania.

Cradle Mountain rises over 5,000 feet and is a hiker's paradise. It takes six to eight days to complete the course and during that time one encounters a host of wild life. There are carnivorous animals like the Tasmanian Devil, a savage, fearsome-looking beast that sleeps by day and attacks the farmers sheep and poultry by night. There are wallabies and echidnas, platypus, and wombats that are nocturnal and easily tameable. One joined us for a while and we called him Willie.

Three types of snakes live in the park and all are venomous, so we had to be cautious and watch where we were walking at all times.

The aroma of food cooking greeted us at each stopover and by the light of the candles, we sat around the log fires and became acquainted with each new host. My favourite host was an Austrian who had a pet wombat and Tom followed us about like a little dog! When we had finished our evening meal Ernst played his Tyrolean tunes on his piano accordion and we all sang. It was a happy, loving experience and none of us could see the dark cloud on the horizon.

We slept in rudimentary huts and the nights were damp and cold, but with the logs provided we stoked up the fire, put our sleeping bags on the floor and slept soundly.

Rising early in the morning, a low mist hung over the marshy bog, clumps of round button grass stood silent, like stepping stones beckoning us onward. In the swirling mist the trees became grotesque and mysterious, the sun's slanting rays cast eeriness and everywhere was hushed.

Preparing our knapsacks for the last time we suddenly realized Daphne was nowhere to be seen. How could she have just vanished? We called, and our voices echoed back to us. We each searched in a different direction. I hastened around the corner and saw her leaning against the wall looking as white as a ghost.

Daphne seemed to be in a state of shock and unwilling to talk. She rapidly worsened and collapsed in a coma before we could get help and was taken to the Royal Hobart Hospital. By then, it was all too late.

Daphne had been bitten on her bottom by a snake. She was ashamed and overcome with false modesty, and rather than confide in any of us, she had allowed herself to die.

A True Story

A Christmas Trilogy

Christmas was always such a happy festive season. My early Christmases were spent in England where there were great expectations of snow and Santa and stockings and going to church with my father and singing carols. Afterward returning to a feast of turkey and all the joys of Christmas fare round the log fire. To me Christmas was a cold country festivity.

When my children were young we celebrated in a hot country. We arrived as emigrants in December, the hottest time of the year and I was surprised to find that Australians ate hot turkey and plum pudding. The thought of cooking all that food in over 100 degree temperatures was almost my undoing. I thought there has to be a better way. I sweated over the preparations, set the timer on the stove and went to bed a little after midnight. Each time the timer sounded I staggered sleepily to the kitchen and basted the turkey, topped up the water in the saucepan to save the pudding from going dry and hoped that God was looking after everything as I crept back into my bed. It was more good luck than judgment that the food was cooked to perfection. We set the trestle tables in the garden under the trees and ate smorgasbord fashion. It was a very happy time. Neighbours joined us and we shared everything with the family and I realized that Christmas in a hot country could also be fun in a different kind of way.

But my most memorable Christmas was when we moved to Brisbane in Queensland, even closer to the equator. We couldn't eat under the trees because it was too hot outside, but we had a large home surrounded by a six foot wide veranda supported by fifteen foot high stumps; a typical old Queensland home raised to keep the house cool. It overlooked the Brisbane River and we did all our entertaining on the veranda, the perfect place with the perfect view.

We arrived in December and I had everything prepared. The cake was made but not decorated when I went into hospital to have my fourth baby. My little Nicholas was born on December 15, 1952.

Christmas Eve our new neighbours called to make our acquaintance. I wished they would soon leave but as they showed no sign of doing so I withdrew to the kitchen as I still had not decorated the cake.

I prepared the ingredients and inadvertently spilt the salt over the table and onto the floor. It was a bad omen and I should have found the time to clear it up.

Instead, I slipped and my head caught the edge of the table. John, my husband, rushed in to see what had happened and found me in a heap on the floor. He helped me onto a chair with my head on the table resting on a bed of towels while he stitched the top of my ear back into place, after sterilizing a darning needle in boiling water. Christmas morning the bandages were removed and my hair carefully arranged to hide the ravages of the night before.

The smorgasbord feast was served with tropical fruits of all kinds from the garden; there were papaws served with ice cream instead of plum pudding, citrus fruit cocktails, and bowls of sweet smelling passion flower blossoms for decoration on the tables. The cake never was decorated but no one seemed to notice.

How I Quit Smoking:

$\mathcal{L}$ike many others I started smoking during the war. When the war ended and my husband was demobilized we emigrated to Australia.

Australians are sociable people, and as newcomers we were invited to numerous parties; dinner parties, cocktail parties, Sunday morning parties beneath the trees in the garden, and almost everyone smoked.

When my husband and I were hosting, little containers with cigarettes were placed strategically throughout our home and we gave little or no thought as to what it might be doing to us.

When I realized the hazards I decided to quit the habit.

But how? It was after dinner at night I craved that cigarette

"It might be a good idea to take the dog for a walk," I told myself. De Grood was our beautiful black Labrador and as our garden opened into a park, I resolved to walk the urge away. I wandered through the trees with Groody scampering along beside me and listened to the rauous laughter of the kookaburras, the song of the magpies, and how they sang; they warbled, and my imagination soared as I blew all the cigarettes into the clouds and visualized them floating away.

Groody became accustomed to his nightly walk and in the end it was Groody that took me! If I sat in a chair even briefly he came to me and plopped his lovely head on my lap, and wagged his tail, an invitation l could not refuse. It was he who helped me succeed.

A Missive From The Pages Of My Diary:

$\mathcal{D}$ear De Grood,

I miss you. I miss you more than you will ever know.

I miss our walks through the forest trails.

And do you remember the gate that lead from our garden into park in Melbourne, and the walks we enjoyed before settling in for the night?

Do you remember the man who hid in the shadows?

We were returning from our walk that evening, and as we neared home you moved close beside me. A low growl rumbled gently within you and the hair on your back bristled.

I couldn't see anything or anyone, but you could. Do you remember that Groody?

Our street was lined with lilly pilly trees. Thick, glossy foliage cast dark shadows across the pavement. You continued to stay close to me and as we neared home you move slowly ahead until, hiding away in the shadows was a tall heavily built man. You went to him, bared your teeth and growled. Not a gentle rumble, but a loud threatening warning.

I walked past the man while you kept guard. You wouldn't let him move and remained crouched, ready to pounce, until I reached home. At the gate I turned to you and called. You looked at the man, gave a loud threatening bark and bounded home to me.

I'm glad you were with me that night, Groody. You probably saved my life.

You looked so sad when I went away. Wherever I walked in Canada I could hear you beside me, but you were not there, it was all a figment of my imagination.

When I left home you went to live with Nick, my son. On his return from work one afternoon, you were missing.

He called, but you did not hear. Nick searched and after awhile he found you in the gutter. You had been hit and killed by a car. Nick was very unhappy. He carried you home and laid you to rest under the tall eucalyptus tree where the magpies used to sing, and planted some daffodils. Now each year in the springtime, there is a carpet of gold to immortalize you. "Goodbye Groody," my dear faithful companion.

A Conundrum:

The trees were shrouded in mist and silent, as dusk descended upon the hills. A dull thud against the fly screen door arrested my attention. I peeped out and there he was! "Hello, Little One!" I said.

His dark brown eyes focused fearlessly on me. Gently I opened the door while speaking quietly to him. He sniffed my shoes and ankles and allowed me to touch his soft warm body covered in brown fur from the tip of his tail to the tips of his ears and whiskers. Little One was fragrant with the aromatic scent of the forest; earthy and fresh, and shining with dew.

When we moved to the hills de Grood, my black Labrador dog, and I, used to walk the trails, and at the bottom of the property was a creek with tree ferns growing on either side, creating a canopy under which we often walked. On the far side of the stream was a burrow in the bank that fascinated Groody; he was in a fervour of excitement whenever we were in the area and try as he might, the entrance that led to the dark mysterious cavern was too small for him to wriggle through. Frustrated, he forsook his quest and bounded through the ferns and bushes to find me.

But that did not stop Groody thinking about him. He wondered what lived there. The scent that emanated from somewhere below, and beyond his reach was unlike anything he knew, and it excited him to a frenzy.

I was about to go to bed that evening when Little One appeared. De Grood was away following his own pursuits, which allowed me time to tempt Little One with food. I offered him bread and milk, dog food, bits of meat and cheese, but he regarded me with disdain and shuffled off into the realms of the eucalypts.

A naturalist lived nearby; he told me that this little animal was a root eater. "Try chopping up some fruit and vegetables," he said. That was the solution! I also learnt that this small friendly animal, with squat legs and stocky body was nocturnal, which is why we had not seen him on our rambles.

What was he?

Few of my readers will know the answer to my conundrum! I will tell them! He was a wombat. Wombats live in southern Australia and on the island of Tasmania.

Over The Moonbi Range:

As a small boy Clavering used to go riding with his father nearly every Sunday. They rode for the most part silently, content with each other's compan, or absorbed in their thoughts. There were several roads that led away from the town in various directions, but the one that the boy liked best was the red and dusty Corrinda road that wound between the wire fences about one hundred yards apart. They could ride for miles this way under the blazing sun without meeting man or beast, and the boy felt akin to the loneliness that seemed to enwrap this silent land in an embrace. And this too was the way to the hills. He never spoke to anyone, not even his father, about the hills which he always thought of as the Moonbi Range, because he liked the sound of the name which he had come across somewhere or other.

After they had ridden some miles, the trees would begin to thin out until there was only a solitary gnarled specimen here and there, that looked as if it had been forgotten by some lone clearer of the land who had long, since departed. And then the hills would appear, mysterious and vast, like a purple fold to the edge of the world. For the boy they held enchantment. There were dragons there, he knew, and was afraid. But even so they called him with a peculiar insistent call, as if together they shared some old sad secret which he had forgotten. He felt quite sure, however, much more sure than he was of the dragons, that there in the heart of his Moonbi Range, if he could only reach it, he would find some unutterable beauty.

Forty years vanished into the past; many of them years of war and death or destruction of which Clavering had seen his share and travelled thousands of miles in the seeing. But now he lay on his beach towel contentedly absorbing the warmth of the sun. His hair had become grey, and the fantasies of his boyhood had disappeared from his memory long ago.

The sun shone from a pale blue sky that was quite clear except for a small bank of cloud low on the eastern horizon. A light warm breeze lazily moved the thin leaves of the casuarina tree which leaned towards the sea, partly shading the tall slim girl who lay face down on her towel beside him. The boat which had brought them to the beach, floated calmly between the rocky horns of the bay, close to the shore. Small groups of gaily clad sunbathers, who had also been rowed over from the main island, lay idly about.

Clavering turned to look at the girl by his side and as if conscious of his regard she suddenly opened her eyes. "Talk to me," she said. Clavering smiled at her. "To the best of my knowledge" he said, "there are only two subjects that interest your sex; clothes and men, and all I know about clothes is that they are things people wear to cover their nakedness." She made a face at him. "Do we really seem to you as bad as all that?" she asked. "Tell me about men then." So he told her tales about men he had known or heard about. Tales of war and peace, of victory and defeat, of hopes and love.

She listened quietly for the most part and the day passed quickly, for though normally he was a quiet man and spoke little, Clavering could talk well when in the mood. He was surprised how quickly the time had gone, and he noticed that the boat which was to take them back to the main island for dinner, was being made ready for departure. The sun was low down and would soon disappear behind one of the islands that dotted the surface of the sea, and a light breeze had sprung up making the beach cool and causing the sunbathers scattered about to put on their clothes.

The girl was sitting with her knees drawn up to her chin, looking out across the blueness of the bay. Suddenly she spoke to him without turning her head, "What", she asked, "is your definition of love?" Clavering was taken by surprise and felt something of the same small shock he had experienced when an examiner had asked him a question for which he did not know the answer. "I don't know," he said, "I don't really know. I haven't got a definition." "But you must know something about love!" she said. "Well, yes, I suppose so," he said. "If you must know I should say that Shelley got as close to it as anybody when he called it "the desire of the moth for the star."

Suddenly her mood changed as she jumped to her feet saying   quite gaily, "Well I am Freudian - everything is sex."

"Good heavens!" he said, "you don't look it," and they both laughed. She was still smiling as hand-in-hand they hurried back to the boat.

"Why all the questions?" he asked. "I wanted to find out something about you" she said, "after all we only met this morning."

After dinner, Clavering was engaged in the usual desultory conversation over a drink, while he waited with the other guests to be drawn out of the hat for the table tennis competition, which was to fill in the evening. He was rather irritated by a vague feeling of dissatisfaction as if he had forgotten something that was important. Hang it all, he thought. What's the matter? I haven't had a holiday like this for years and I want to enjoy every minute of it, and he gave a small shrug of his shoulders as he walked from the bar towards the table tennis room where he would watch and play in the competition. As the names were called out, the competition was for mixed doubles, men and girls took their places and faced each other at opposite ends of the rather battered table. Names did not mean anything to Clavering. He did not know any of their names and he watched the progress of the games idly and without much interest, for the standard of play, so far, had been poor. His interest quickened, however, as more names were called, and he noticed the girl who had spent the day on the beach with him standing with her partner waiting to begin another round. He was slightly annoyed that he had missed the names as they were called out until he realized it wouldn't have made any difference, just the name and initial were called. Not Mr. or Mrs. or Miss. In any case what did it matter, the girl would be gone and forgotten in a couple of days. All the same he liked her and hoped she would win. He leaned slightly forward as the game began. She played easily and quickly and was obviously at home with ball games. It seemed to Clavering that there was something gallant about her. She had drawn a good partner and they played through to the final.

When the entertainment was ended and the party began to break up, Clavering walked across the room to where she was sitting. "Bed time?" he asked. "I think so," she said. "You did very well, with a bit of luck at the finish I think you would have won the final." "Thank you," she said, "But they really were much better than we were." She rose from her seat. "I'll walk with you down to the cabin," he said, "it's only a little way." They walked together beneath the coconut palms that lined the path. It was very quiet. "I hear we are being taken to one of the island reefs tomorrow. Will you come with me?" he said. "I would love to," she replied. "Look," he said, "it will be a fine day tomorrow. See the stars are shining. You can see the Southern Cross between the leaves of that palm tree," and he pointed overhead and to the right.

The outline of her face was reflected softly by the light of the stars, as she lifted her head towards them, and Clavering was suddenly seized with an almost uncontrollable desire to take her in his arms. It was not passion. Clavering knew something about passion. It was more the feeling, the tenderness one has for a lost child, or an old friend. It seemed so completely natural as if he had always known her.

"Good God," he thought. "Yesterday I didn't even know she existed. I still don't even know her name. She'd be quite certain she was dealing with a maniac. Good night," he said abruptly, "see you tomorrow," and he hurried to his cabin.

The following day was clear and fine, but a strong wind had arisen overnight and the 'Shangri-la' dipped her bows into the waves and flung the spray high as she carried them around the island to spend the morning at a reef in a sheltered bay some miles away. They sat together in the stern of the boat, partly sheltered from the wind by a canvas awning, feeling the rise and fall of the sea and watching the islands as they came and went. A flock of gulls followed always on the wings of the wind behind them, searching for scraps of food with intent eyes that missed nothing. "Is it true that you are leaving us tomorrow?" he asked. "Yes," she said, "I'm afraid I must. My holiday is nearly over." "In that case then would you do me a last favour? "After lunch, when we get back from the reef, will you walk with me to the other side of the island where we can lie on the beach, away from the wind. We have very little time left and I should like to spend it with you. It's not far, only about a mile."

The path across the island to Coconut Bay wound in easy grades between eucalyptus and pine trees until they reached the bay, and sat down together on the beach.

After a few minutes Clavering spoke. " Yesterday, I told you some tales of men and places I had known. Today it is your turn. Tell me a little about yourself; about the things you have liked and done." So he heard about her childhood in the Kentish marshes where she was born within sound of the sea and the cry of the gulls flying overhead. She told him that when in Switzerland she had climbed the Matterhorn. Clavering waved his hand towards his forehead. "Madam, I salute you," he said. "Not even after a full bottle of whisky could I even think of trying to climb the Matterhorn, assuming, of course, that I could think at all." They talked then to each other of their lives and the circumstances of their lives with the easy sureness of complete understanding until it was time to return. Later that evening Clavering walked with her beneath the coconut palms to her cabin. The stars continued to shine and this time Clavering took her in his arms and kissed her goodnight.

CANDI

Turning Point:

It was September when we camped our way through the Rocky Mountains.

The snow line crept down the slopes and we had finished our evening meal. The squirrels and the chipmonks joined us and the occasional deer peeped shyly, with one leg poised, as though ready for flight.

We sat around the log fire for the last time. The flames and sparks leapt towards the stars, our hands cupped round our hot rums and the delicious sweet aroma lingered on the night air. Peace was everywhere. We did not speak, we did not want to break the silence or disturb the memories. It had been a holiday of consequence and I knew, one day, I would return.

That was when my turning point was born, but it did not become reality until four years later, when I closed my door for the very last time.

Thus it came about that I left the heat of an Australian summer and arrived in Canada in the middle of winter. I flew into Vancouver on a cold dreary day. I was tired and emotionally spent.

It had been a long and tedious journey but after a good night's sleep I felt infused with the spirit of confidence; the content of my life was now dominated by what was, rather than by what had been, and there was no turning back.

My Canadian Odyssey

A freak thunderstorm hit Melbourne closing Tullarmarine airport, halting city traffic and flooding country roads. That was the beginning of my Canadian odyssey. We had driven in the blinding rain to the airport. My family and friends came to see me off and as I turned and waved I felt sorrow, and wondered when I would see any of them again.

January 14 1977:

All flights were delayed and disrupted by the storm. I wrote in my diary: It was a rough flight. We kept our seat belts on and no refreshments were served as we bounced our way to Sydney, and when the plane dropped my stomach felt suspended in space. I think it was the roughest flight of my life. We landed at midnight, five hours late. It was raining heavily and there were no taxis or porters but eventually a cab came and I was taken to the Gemini Motel.

January 15/77:

It seemed I had only just fallen into bed when the wake up call came, I dressed hurriedly and took the elevator to the lobby. It was still dark but the motel shuttle-bus was waiting. I, and the other passengers, were taken to the airport terminal in plenty of time and checked in. Breakfast was served soon after take-off. We flew via Nadi and Honolulu and touched down in both countries where we waited in selected areas, like cattle in a holding pen, I thought. As we neared Vancouver I looked through the window of the DC8 and viewed the snow-capped mountains, my heart was filled with wonder and joy. We had crossed the international date line and flown through two time zones, flying back in time and it was still January 15 1977, twenty four hours later.

Ray, my daughter, met me at the airport. It was wonderful to see her waiting there. We stayed at the Grosvenor Hotel, in Vancouver. There was much to talk about and tough decisions had to be made. Ray was my sponsor and therefore responsible for me. I was not prepared for what had taken place two months earlier. It was November 1976. The Australian dollar had been devalued and I was advised to leave my money until the dollar recovered. When the time came and I applied to the Reserve Bank, they refused my application. Time had expire, I had waited too long. I had no alternative but to work. I was not young enough to break into the clerical field with all its word processors and computers. Besides, I had not worked in an office for many years, during that time everything had completely changed.

Ray, always level-headed, said, "Don't worry about it now, Mother, recover from the journey and let's enjoy our few days together." I accepted her advice and we left the Grosvenor Hotel and drove to Tsawwassen and took the ferry to Swartz Bay on Vancouver Island. We had breakfast on the Queen of Alberni. The sun streamed through the lounge windows and scenically it was beautiful as we plied our way between the Gulf islands. As we sat there together studying maps, and pamphlets for accommodation, a gentleman stopped beside us and asked if he could assist us. I knew by his voice that he was an Australian. When he realized I was a new emigrant he offered all the help he could. Solicitor, friends, telephone numbers, and asked me to call him at his Salt Spring Island home later that evening. He was retired and elderly and had immigrated to Canada many years ago. He had been educated at Scotch College in Melbourne, the same school that Graham, one of my sons had attended. He was kind and we kept in touch until his death on his ninetieth birthday.

Ray and I booked into the Daffodil Motel on Douglas Street, not far from the city centre. I liked Victoria, British Columbia's capital. I thought it a fascinating city with quaint streets and shops and likened it to Hobart, Tasmania's capital, both have deep-water harbours. I thought how lovely it would be to live there.

For several days Ray and I drove around the island. We parked the car near bays and coves and walked along the sandy beaches. I loved it from the very beginning. We drove over the Mallahat Pass and had lunch in a restaurant with breathtaking views across the water and mountains. And one sunny morning we went to the Butchardt Gardens and enjoyed a smorgasbord meal and listened to an open-air concert by the Canadian Scottish Pipers.

Another interesting episode happened while we were together.

I knew I had a cousin in Canada and I thought he lived somewhere on the prairies. We decided to check the telephone directory and were astonished to find him listed in Victoria. We had finished dinner and it was a lovely evening and on the spur of the moment we drove round, and with the aid of a street map we found where the Lofts lived. Beatrice opened the door, she thought we were selling encyclopaedias! But when I said Alfred's father and my mother were brother and sister, the statement made quite an impact and we were welcomed with drinks and much bonhomie.

Alfred was a Professor of English Literature at the University of Victoria and Bea, a golf and garden enthusiast. After our first meeting we wined and dined together often, familiarizing ourselves with each other. It was good to know we had relatives in Victoria and it gave me a sense of belonging.

Ray's time was running out but before leaving she suggested we call at the Red Cross. Dear girl, so kind and helpful. When we reached the office I asked if they could use me? "I need a bed, a roof over my head, and I need it now!" I couldn't believe my luck. I had my first job. I was to commence the following day. I was given two pale blue uniforms with fine white cotton aprons, and told to buy towels and face cloths. Ray and I left feeling jubilant. Ray had to return to Kamloops but before leaving Victoria she drove me to see where I would be spending the next six weeks. During that time I cared for a man with Alzheimer's disease while his wife visited her family and friends in England. It gave me the experience I needed and was the beginning of My Canadian Odyssey.

An Ode To
A Remarkable Man

We met on the ferry soon after my arrival in Canada. I knew he was a diabetic but he loved his food, and sometimes I used to shudder at the things he ate with complete abandon and relish.

He and his wife left the scenic and remote Saltspring Island and moved to Nanaimo. They bought a home overlooking the water and mountains. There was a bald eagle rookery in the trees nearby and deer wandered freely, all so peaceful and picturesque.

They had not been there long when he was taken to the hospital with a sore toe. He was given insulin and although they managed to stabilize the diabetes he had to have one of his legs amputated.

When I visited him in hospital he was sitting up in bed looking extremely well. He threw out his arms in welcome saying, "Aren't I lucky, I still have one leg left."

Not long afterwards he was hospitalized for the last time. He said to his wife, "If they should ring you in the night to tell you I have gone, rejoice with me." He died peacefully in his sleep that same evening.

A truly remarkable man.

An Awakening

*N*ight after night I lay awake, rearranged my pillows but still sleep eluded me. The children were asleep and my husband beside me, even the cat and dog slept curled up together; but I had forgotten how.

That was a long time ago. Now the children were married, and I widowed. While making toast I thought about that night and all the other nights I had lain there without sleeping. My bed was comfortable, chosen with care. The covers matched the curtains, muted pastel, soothing shades, conducive to sleep. When daylight peeped through the window I slept drowsily, briefly.

I finished my breakfast and looked at myself in the mirror. I was tall, thin and lissom. My hair was grey but it suited me, I told myself. No longer did I have to rush off to the office, and soon spring would return, the evenings lengthen and I would be able to walk, hike the mountain trails and travel. I had retired and felt free at last.

But that day it was wet and cheerless and I was feeling sorry for myself for no particular reason. "I'll switch the radio on, there might be something interesting," I said aloud. I often talked to myself now that I lived alone.

I heard a man saying, "After thirty years I am now able to sleep." I was immediately alert and when the announcer said there was to be an introductory lecture that evening I made up my mind to be present.

I arrived at the hotel and after making enquiries found my way to the lecture room. Even though I was early, the room was already crowded with men and women of all ages and from widely varying backgrounds; doctor's secretaries, teachers, housewives, business people and teenagers. A man greeted me and found me a seat. I squeezed between them and sat down.

When Dino arrived the lights were dimmed and he told the audience to close their eyes. We were guided through a series of exercises into a state of deep relaxation.

It gave me a feeling of weightlessness. I could not feel myself. I was floating and was sorry when we were told to wake up. It was not really sleep, but a happy suspension of thought.

The audience was invited to speak about their problems. I spoke about my sleeping disorder and was surprised to discover there were many others like me.

Meditation followed. Dino guided us. During that time we had to take our pulse while thinking of something pleasant. I walked around the Lost Lagoon in the darkness of my mind and my pulse was perfectly normal. But when the experience was repeated while thinking of something traumatic that had happened during our lifetime, my pulse almost doubled. I had performed the miracle, without the help of anyone, just the memory of things past. Surely, if I could do that to myself, I could overcome my inability to sleep.

Dino discussed sleeplessness and dreams, lack of concentration, and pain, which, he claimed, could all be cured through meditation. I was convinced and signed up for the full course.

When the lecture ended I slipped quietly away. It was a beautiful starlight night, close to midnight. Someone offered me a lift home but I declined, I wanted to walk and to be alone, to reflect upon all that had happened and to savour what I had experienced.

Reaching my apartment I hurriedly undressed and sank to the floor amongst some pillows. I wanted to experiment, to meditate without the vibrations of the other people.

I found a comfortable position and closed my eyes, took a deep breath and began the mind control exercises I had just learnt. I found myself, once again, slipping into the same trance-like sensation of floating, before getting into bed and sleeping for ten glorious hours.

In the morning I felt rejuvenated and revitalized. It had changed my whole life. It gave me an inner peace and awakened powers in me that I did not know I had.

I sat up and stretched, threw out my arms to embrace the new day and looked through the window to the mountains beyond, covered in a new dusting of snow. I inhaled deeply with contentment. Life is good, I must dress and get out into the morning air; I slept! I slept! How good it is to be alive.

* *

With the passage of time and with each new day, I continue to wander down the path of self-discovery and in the words of William Blake:

> *I see a world in a grain of sand*
> *And a heaven in a wild flower,*
> *Hold infinity in the palm of my hand*
> *And eternity in an hour.*

$\mathcal{GRIEF}$ October 1991

$\mathcal{T}$his was written after receiving a letter from my brother, telling me that his grandson had died.

And I wandered along the seawall seeking some words of comfort and solace to send them, but found none. We all suffer grief throughout our lives and although the hurt and sorrow may lessen I don't believe it ever goes away. But what is grief and how do we cope with it? My mother died during the war and a few weeks later my fiancé was killed in action.

I couldn't cry, but some mornings when I awoke my pillow was wet with my tears.

Bombs continued to fall and more people were killed, causing endless, senseless, suffering. We all silently grieved with each other but no one spoke of it, just a look or a glance of understanding was enough.

Grief though, can mean different emotions for people.

My sister's younger son was killed in a motorbike accident when he was nineteen. His father was so distraught he suffered a stroke, and died soon afterwards. Molly, however, remained calm and inscrutable throughout the ordeal and when I asked her the secret of her self control and apparent happiness she replied simply, "You don't understand, life is just beginning."

I wished I had had her faith. Death and grief are synonymous with one another leaving for me, an unfillable void, forever.

TO MY NEPHEW PETER:

I miss you,
I think of you often,
The pain and suffering.
The motorbike you were riding
To work one morning and
The lorry that turned
The corner but did not see you.
Your back was broken.
You did not lose consciousness
And were hospitalized
For ten long days
Before you went to sleep
And did not wake up.
So I write this in memory
Of a dear nephew, aged nineteen.

Joan Woodley

It Is All Or Nothing

Thursday was one of those days when everything I touched felt cold, even Angela, my little typewriter felt cold. I put on my leg- warmers and wrapped a shawl around my shoulders. I wanted to type but my fingers weren't working very well so I added some mittens.

I looked through the window across the tops of the cottages. Smoke spiralled from some of the chimneys, new snow had fallen in the night and the mountains beyond were lost in mist. It was minus four degrees.

I had lived in my apartment since July and even though the thermostat registered ninety degrees, I had no heat. I had already mentioned it to the manager but it had fallen on deaf ears so I wrote him a note and popped it under the office door: "Tom, I am cold, Please fix my heat!"

Soon afterwards he arrived. Tom walked in with a disarming smile saying, "I thought I'd fixed it!" "No such luck," I replied. "You talked about flushing out the pipes to let the hot water flow through, but you didn't return."

He took the covers off the heaters in the living room and bedroom. Pulled my bed and the bedside table away from the wall and left them in the middle of the room, promising to return the next day.

Early evening I turned on my electric blanket and allowed an hour to elapse before filling my hot water bottle; at least I could be warm in bed. As I got in between the sheets I was perplexed and not a little annoyed to see water seeping out of my hot-water bottle.

I stripped the bed. The sheets I put aside, but the mattress would have to wait. I arranged cushions and pillows on the floor and slept fitfully.

The next day Tom returned bringing with him a collection of mechanical devices and a long hose. I suppose he spent an hour hammering and suctioning out the dirt before replacing the covers over the heaters and vacuuming the carpet. Tom left everything neat and tidy and replaced my bed and bedside table with TLC; he adjusted the thermostat on the wall and departed.

"At last," I said aloud, "how lovely to be warm!" But the irony of it all; I feel I am living in a hothouse; I cannot turn off the heat! It is all; or nothing!

Stranger Than Fiction:

I was in Safeway at the checkout; a few people in front of me, a young man behind me. Pleasant chap.

He looked clean but unshaven. I thought, he is either letting his beard grow or, he is a scruffy fellow. Fiddling with my change I dropped two pennies. The young man had his hands full of groceries but he stopped the pennies with his foot. I thanked him and picked them up. All I had was a birthday card. I handed it to the teller, she put it in a bag and passed it back to me.

"But I haven't paid for it!" I said, "He has" said she. I turned around to the young man, "But you can't do that," I said. "Yes, I can, and I have." I waited for him to go through the checkout, and said, "You'll go to heaven! ""Have a good day," he replied, and we both smiled at one another.

* * * * * * * * * * * * * * * * * *

I was in the local grocery store. It was September, the first bitterly cold day, the wind straight off the ocean. In the store I heard a strange sound. I became curious and followed it. There was a young girl wearing shorts, nothing on her feet or legs, and a short-sleeved tee shirt. In her arms she had a wee baby wrapped in cotton blanket. I followed her to the checkout. She bought three plums and a carton of milk and paid with fiver dollar note. Once in the Mall she sat on a seat, opened the carton of milk and poured it down the babies throat causing the poor wee thing to choke. I didn't wait but rushed home, dialled 911 and as soon as the phone was picked up I said, "I don't want any of things you are going to ask me, but this is what has happened!" Before, I had finished, she said, "It's alright, someone is on the way!"

* * * * * * * * * * * * * * * * * * * *

It was Christmastime and I was waiting for the bus to take me home with a few other people, every one cheery and wishing each other Christmas Greetings. A lady walking briskly joined us. She was happy and smiling and joined in the bonhomie when suddenly she fell to the ground. A young man rushed across the road to the nearest shop and called an ambulance. But by then it was all too late. In the midst of life we are in death, I thought. What, I wonder, does happen to us afterwards.

> ... acceptance is a feeling of victory,
> a feeling of peace, of serenity,
> of positive submission of things
> we cannot change.

One Woman's Knitting Bag:

$\mathcal{S}$he was going off to Reno for Christmas, to try her luck, and to escape from her small apartment.

The only thing Marjorie had ever won in her life was a knitting bag in a raffle. As she did not knit she used it for odds and ends.

Popping a cheese sandwich into her knitting bag one day Marjorie wandered to the beach and sat in the warm sunshine. She gazed out to sea and reflected dreamily and thought of all the money she hoped to win, and what she would do with it, if only she could be one of the lucky ones.

The waves continued to break on the shore and the peace of her surroundings finally lulled her to sleep.

When she awoke she gazed around with a feeling of contentment and the pangs of hunger made her think of her cheese sandwich.

Marjorie reached for her knitting bag and was surprised to see it moving up and down as though something was inside. She watched intrigued as the rise and fall continued. After a while a gluttonous rat emerged having eaten his way through the bag to the cheese and was now complacently looking at her, as much as to say, 'thank you,' before scurrying off into the shelter of some logs to sleep off his ill-gotten gains!

My Home; My View

*R*ecently I moved into a high-rise in Vancouver's West End. It is 26 storeys high, and I live on the 18th floor overlooking Stanley Park. The building is octagonal in shape and each suite has a blue painted balcony.

Having lived in a bachelor for the past 5 years it is like a palace! The rooms are light and airy with plenty of space, and the view defies description.

I have placed my desk, supposedly set aside in an area for dining, so that I can gaze through the French windows to the panoramic vista of the park, the waterfront, and the mountains beyond, and on a clear sunny day Vancouver Island is silhouetted on the skyline. The sun sets immediately behind the island and a new painting is born.

Looking out of my window and viewing the trees from above, I have a totally different perspective of their shapes and shades. Some rounded, some pointed and reaching towards the sky, and the reds and golds interspersed with the many greens create a kaleidoscopic view of the whole. The scene is ever changing and new paintings are being formed. Sometimes there are wisps of low cloud swirling in and out of the trees and sometimes I am buried in cloud and can see nothing at all.

It is beautiful to watch the birds. With each new day they come they soar, they glide above the treetops, always hungry, always looking for food but always gliding with outstretched wings as though they hadn't a care in the world. How wonderful it would be if we could emulate the birds and allow the wind to carry us along on it's current, how much more peaceful the universe would be.

I spend many a lone hour seated at my desk; I talk to it, but it doesn't answer me. So I enjoy the silence writing, dreaming, and thinking. Sometimes, I just sit in reverie and ponder the past, and the future.

Joan Woodley 1992

Spring, In The Autumn Of Life:

I helped Freddie into his wheel chair and pushed him into the garden. The azaleas and rhododendrons were in bloom; it was a lovely day. The blue sky with wisps of white clouds scudded away into the distance, the swiftly flowing water of the canyon rushed headlong towards the ocean; a constant accompaniment to the song of the robins. Winter had passed.

We found our sequoia tree. It was a favourite haunt of ours. I adjusted Freddie's pillows, covered his legs with a rug, and kissed him lightly. Throwing some cushions onto the grass, I used the buttressed trunk of the old tree for a backrest, and enjoyed the fragrant scent of cedar. In my pocket I had a diary and I began to read.

We met in the bank! There was the usual line-up. In front of me was a tall fair man and as the queue moved slowly I became curious. He had fine physique. Was he good-looking? How old was he? Those were the questions turning over in my mind. As if by telepathy, he turned and smiled at me. I smiled back. We talked about the slowly moving people ahead of us, the weather, and other inconsequential snippets of conversation, and as we neared the tellers, he turned and smiled at me and said, "Let's have some coffee together?" I nodded my assent.

When the tellers had finished with us we walked to a nearby cafe. We found a seat by the window overlooking English Bay and watched the yachts with their white sails dancing in the wind. There was a stiff breeze and the water choppy, a perfect day for sailing. "Would you like to be out there?" he said. "Oh, yes," I replied.   "I had a boat once, but that was a long time ago, when I lived in South Africa." Then he spoke about his early life in Holland, where he grew up on his father's farm, the war years in England, followed by a stint in Cape Town before finally settling in Canada.

We prepared to leave the cafe when he stopped and looked at me; "I don't know your name," he said. "I don't know yours either," I replied, and we both laughed. We introduced ourselves and left the cafe hand-in-hand. Freddie had an appointment and I wandered home. A chance encounter had suddenly brought this man into my life; was he married, I wondered, would he call me as he said he would?

The evening dragged on and my mind was like a grasshopper flitting from one flower to another, not settling for long on anything and when the sun sank behind the mountains, leaving a crimson glow across the water, I began to prepare for bed. I was about to slip between the sheets when the telephone startled me into consciousness.

I, barely awake was surprised to hear Freddie's voice. "It's a glorious morning! Will you join me for a walk?" "I would love to," I replied.

We walked along Vancouver's waterfront. The early morning sun rose above the mountains and cast a warm glow across the water. All was still.

Few people had left their beds, it was the perfect time to be out. We watched a bald eagle swoop into the water and make a sudden attack on a fish and fly with it into the distance. And, a young mole, lost, and almost blind, unable to find his way across the path. We held his little warm furry body and put him gently on a mound of soil and hoped he would be able to find his way underground.

As we walked along the seawall Freddie talked to me and all the questions that had been floating around in my head were answered. His wife had died after a prolonged illness. He had two children, a son and a daughter and four grandsons.

When we reached the Tea House we stopped for breakfast. We ate outside in the garden under the striped umbrellas overlooking the ocean, and watched the freighters coming and going to we knew not where. It was as Freddie had said, a glorious morning, and the beginning of a beautiful relationship. We walked often, went to concerts, dined and danced, and Freddie taught me to play golf.

We spent many happy holidays together touring Vancouver Island and the Oregon Coast.

But, I think, one of our happiest holidays was hiking the Cariboo and Chilcotin Country in the centre of British Columbia.

You Pass This Way But Once:

$\mathcal{A}$s the train pulled away from the station I watched the crowds growing smaller. With hat in hand, Freddie waved, until he faded into the distance and disappeared altogether. Suddenly I felt very alone. It was an emotion that washed over me like a wave.

A coloured Porter showed me to my small, but compact compartment. My bed, that doubled as a sofa by day was comfortable, with snowy white linen. For a few minutes I gazed at the passing scene; how drear it was! The Indian Reserve, some dilapidated houses and a light rain splashed the window. I swayed my way along the corridor to the dining car and felt a mixture of excitement and apprehension, and wondered what the future had in store for me.

I enjoyed Canadian salmon, followed by strawberry mousse, and after coffee I returned to my **roomette**.

Clambering into my bed I quickly became accustomed to the motion and rattle of the train and slept soundly. In the morning the sun was shining. My world contrasted dramatically with the previous night. We were crossing the Rocky Mountains as I took my place in the observatory coach. A lady came along. We smiled, she asked if she could join me? "Yes, of course," I replied. We soon got into conversation as I heard about her daughter who lived in Toronto and she was on her way to visit her. "What about you, where are you going?" "Toronto," I replied. I was glad of her company; she was cheerful and her happiness was infectious.

As we neared Jasper, with cameras clicking, we absorbed the panoramic splendour of the landscape. We watched as a silver fox streaked by like a graceful gazelle, and a herd of deer stood still, filled with curiosity as the train passed slowly by.

Isabel and I shared many interests, from our Scandinavian ancestors, to our philosophies towards life. I told her of my meeting with Freddie and how he took me to the station. And with hat held high above his head, he waved. I threw him a kiss and called "Goodbye, Freddie!" But it wasn't the end, it was only the beginning." "And now?" Isabel queried? "I haven't a penny, and am working my way across Canada!"

The three days journey passed uneventfully and the train finally pulled into the station in the small hours of the morning disgorging its passengers, a dishevelled looking lot. There was numbness in the air as the people scrambled for their luggage and walked purposefully towards the exit, the only sounds were the tapping of the women's heels and the slamming of carriage doors. Isabel and I were destined to meet again but, of necessity, our paths had to part temporarily, and after a quick wave of the hand, Isabel vanished in the seething mass of humanity.

This was my first visit to Toronto. I felt lost and bewildered as my search for a porter proved useless. I dragged my bags to the taxi rank and waited in the queue. Eventually my turn came and I was taken to the YWCA, which was to be my temporary home.

Once settled I explored Toronto; it was big and impersonal, and why was everybody in such a hurry? I climbed to the top of the Sky Dome, viewed the skyscrapers, Provincial Parliament Buildings, its huge shopping complex, and the sandy peninsula jutting into the lake that helped to form the natural harbour. I bought a copy of The Globe and Mail, Toronto's main daily newspaper, and studied the job vacancies and came across an advertisement for a mature, nature loving person with drivers' licence. I applied, and was accepted, becoming a companion to a lady who could find no one prepared to share her solitary existence in her country home, which was palatial, hidden away in hundreds of acres of forest and miles from anywhere.

Her town home was in Rosedale, an exclusive suburb of Toronto and I soon discovered, that with all her wealth she was an unhappy and embittered woman. After much preparation, the time came for us to leave and I found myself the chauffeuse of a Lincoln Continental. Inwardly I trembled as I had not driven on the 'other' side of the road. We packed everything into the car, including the two black Labrador retriever dogs, and set off.

Away from the city we drove through the picturesque countryside to Uxbridge, a small village with tree-lined streets and homes with lovely colourful gardens.

This was our nearest place to civilization where we could shop for food, and collect our mail and newspapers. Continuing our journey along a gravel road we arrived at 'Frogsmere', in the middle of nowhere. My lady had her own suite and I had mine so we lived relatively separate lives. There was no television, only a little transistor radio to keep us in touch with the outside world. It was utterly remote and as the weeks passed, the last of the snow vanished and everywhere sprang to life. I was astonished at the speed with which everything grew. There were fruit

trees and vegetables that the gardeners looked after, and
as the weeks slipped into months we grew to know, and to
accept each other, but it was beyond me to understand her
moods and irrational behaviour, when she would fly into
a rage, followed by outbursts of tears. The dogs would
cower, and with ears down and tails between their legs
they sought my companionship and we would wander off
for long walks through the glorious property. By the time
we arrived back it was over and forgotten.

Mrs Duc liked to eat out of doors and as the house was
surrounded by a deep overhung verandah we enjoyed
our meals outside. My lady would talk, and I became
the scapegoat for her constant complaints about life and
all the blows it had dealt her. I felt like telling her to look
around and to count her blessings; she was blessed with
so much.

During the hot summer evenings Mrs Duc would lock
herself away in a darkened room and play records of
classical music. I would sit on the verandah and listen,
and to the accompaniment of the frogs that lived in a
nearby pond. I enjoyed the peace of it all and watched
the shadows of the trees spread tracery over the sloping
lawns that tumbled into the lake below. The dogs were
my constant companions and the days passed happily
enough.

Mrs Due enjoyed working in her flower garden and
produced a colourful herbaceous border but sometimes
she seemed so full of anger and ill feeling, I wondered if
in her imagination she was actually attacking someone,
and who that person might be? She was paranoid about
her husband, a Swiss gentleman, who had returned to
Switzerland, taking with him a beautiful young woman,
but that had happened years ago. Now she was a recluse,
hiding herself away from the world. But her bad temper
finally got the better of her. Some irrational impulse made

her go to the tool shed for her spade. She stomped off to the flower garden and thrust it into the soil; watched fascinated. Almost immediately she cried out for help. I rushed to her aid but was unable to move her. Seeking the help of one of the gardeners we half-dragged, half-carried her indoors and up the stairs to her room and on to her bed. With much difficulty I helped her undress and suggested calling the local doctor. But she would have none of it saying, "The local doctors are no good!"

I was in a dilemma. I bought her an electric blanket for comfort. I tried massage and lotions to no avail, she had dislocated her back and there was nothing I could do. It became an intolerable situation until finally she demanded to be taken back to Toronto.

I packed her belongings and mine, stowed them in the Lincoln, put dustsheets over the furniture and returned to Rosedale.

Against her wishes, and while she remonstrated, I dialled 911 and an ambulance arrived and took her to the hospital where, with considerable relief, I left her in the capable hands of the doctors and nurses.

I stayed in the Rosedale home with the dogs until My Lady's daughter arrived a day or two later. I felt curious about Mrs Duc's astonishing behaviour and asked Jane, if her mother was always angry? "Yes, I think she is," was the reply. "She hates men, especially since Dad ran off with another woman; she seems to be disillusioned with life itself. But she loves her garden and her dogs."

'And you pass this way but once', I thought. Then it was time for me to leave. I had played my part. It had been an experience, now it was time to move on and with no misgivings, or regrets, I bade them adieu!

I sent my soul through the invisible
Some letter of that After-life to spell,
And by-and-by my Soul returned to me
And answered, "I myself am Heav'n and Hell"

OMAR KHAYYAM

Christmas In Nova Scotia

$\mathscr{I}$ caught the 11:30 night train. I slept, but fitfully.

As we neared Nova Scotia the sky glowed red and the sun peeped through the early morning mist. The taxi wound its way along the sleepy city streets to the sound of the foghorn and I spent one night at the Chateau Halifax.

After a hot bath I fell, into bed and slept deeply until the alarm woke me. With a sense of excitement I made my way to the restaurant and enjoyed brunch; ham and eggs, fries, toast and coffee.

It was not light enough to see much of Halifax from the windows of the taxi but what I saw I liked. I went to the lobby to book one more night but, to my chagrin they were fully booked and the clerk said, "I don't think you will get in anywhere, a world-wide fishing conference has flooded the small city." She suggested I try the Y, but that too, was fully booked.

I bought a copy of the Halifax Chronicle and returned to my room somewhat chastened by this unexpected turn of events.

Hastily I read the advertisements. Two jobs presented themselves; one with children that had already been taken, and the other a long distance call. The voice on the end of the line sounded pleasant, saying, "I will send my son to interview you."

We met in the lobby of the hotel and after a drink he took me to dinner. I had not enjoyed an interview with dinner before and found it a very pleasant experience. I remember wearing a black slack suit with fitted jacket, and a pink and grey paisley chiffon blouse.

John, my benefactor, was an architect, his father a doctor, and his mother in hospital having suffered a stroke and it would be my job to care for her if I decided to stay. The wine flowed through me and I felt warmth for this young man who had so trustingly accepted me on behalf of his father.

The following day we drove to Bridgewater, a little fishing village in Nova Scotia and I was taken to the local hospital to meet Isabel. We had an immediate rapport. The task ahead was not going to be easy but I felt that together, we would succeed.

The doctor I met later. He was a semi-retired physician who had delivered most of the village children. They worked by barter. He took care of their minor ills and the people brought gifts of chicken, fruit and vegetables. He was a kindly gentleman who enjoyed a good book and a game of chess in his spare time.

They lived in a century-old timber home and I had a complete suite on the top floor overlooking the garden that was large and neglected. Until Isabel came home, having little to do, I cleared the weeds and found rose bushes together with delphiniums and a host of other perennials struggling to reach the sun. I persuaded the doctor to take me to a nearby nursery and we bought a variety of annuals, and with care everything flourished and soon produced a colourful array of flowers. Ben was most impressed! He was no gardener but he arranged for a young lad from the village to cut the lawns.

When Isabel finally returned her face shone with happiness. "What a welcome!" she exclaimed. "I am so happy to be home and I have never seen the garden look more beautiful." Isabel was an artist and there were water colours and oils all over the house, pictures of seascapes and landscapes, birdlife, and rugged fishermen with their nets and trawlers; she had captured the spirit on canvas in all its many moods and her sketches, too, were graphic.

Nova Scotia was an artist's paradise with its many coves and rural countryside, expansive views of picturesque lighthouses that jutted out on to the headlands. In the sunshine it presented a colourful scene but when the relentless, bitter Atlantic storms roared with savage velocity, nothing could have been more desolate and I marvelled at the courage of the lighthouse keepers.

Isable progressed slowly. I took her for walks in her wheelchair but she tired readily and often we sat in the rose garden. She liked to reminisce about her early life and what it was like growing up in a small community in Nova Scotia. Her father wanted her to be a musician but she chose to be an artist and it was her greatest joy just to be able to sketch. Then she broke down and wept wondering if she would ever be able to paint again.

We both enjoyed music and spent many happy hours together listening to her favourite recordings. I read to her and took her to the local library to choose her own books and the days passed as imperceptibly as time itself, from summer and into autumn when the trees turned crimson and gold and displayed all the richness of fall.

The long summer evenings grew shorter and a chill descended upon us before the snow clouds gathered and the first flurries began to swirl through the air. Isabel grew restless. It was too cold to take her for walks. The physiotherapist came regularly but progress was slow.

Ben and I spent long hours discussing the problem until one morning I had a dream. I hurriedly dressed and went to Ben.. "Ben, I have an idea. You have a beautiful home filled with paintings, Isabel's paintings, why not exhibit them?. Let the people come." He didn't reply immediately, then he said, "I think it is a great idea, let's discuss it with Isabel." We sat together around the table and we put the suggestion before her. She was so excited she wanted to start preparing right away. So we drew up a list of people who would be invited and sent invitations to family and friends as far away as Halifax, and to everyone in the local community. Soon the house was filled with enthusiasm and excitement and Isabel found new meaning in living.

As the time drew near we decorated the home with holly and lit the fires. Ben took care of the cocktails and I, the savouries. When the day arrived we wheeled Isabel into mingle with the guests.

She wore a pale blue dress, long to hide the brace on her leg. The hairdresser had called during the morning and her fair hair, flecked with silver, shone like a halo. Fortunately her stroke had not affected her appearance and her speech very little. It was a festive occasion and Isabel loved it. She sold some paintings, and everyone radiated the warmth of love and happiness for her.

With the departure of the last of the guests we went into dinner. During the summer months there were flowers from the garden, and food served at table with wine, but with the coming of Christmas there were candles and holly for decoration.

That evening Ben ate heartily but Isabel, buoyed with excitement, had little appetite.

When the meal was over we returned to the lounge and sat together round the fire. We watched the sparks disappear into the chimney and listened to the friendly crackle of the logs while outside the snowflakes continued to tumble, numbing the sounds of the passing cars and the distant songs of praise of the carollers. We were all reluctant to leave the comfort of the fireside but with the warm glow of the dying embers still upon us we took Isabel to her room and helped her to bed. She was happy. We turned down the light and kissed her goodnight. As we left the room I turned and looked at her; she was at peace.

Ben and I enjoyed a final nightcap and a game of cribbage before we, too, retired. Ben put the guard to the fire, and I fed the cat. The day was complete.

Before going to my room I went in to see if Isabel needed anything. She was surrounded by an aura of tranquility. But as I looked at her, I became afraid, and crept closer. I listened, but could hear nothing. Nothing but the ticking of the clock on her bedside table. Tears sprang to my eyes as I realized I had lost the Isabel I had grown to love.

Some months later I arrived in Banff and found Deer Lodge, an alpine chalet in the mountains and joined a group of hikers. Each day we climbed the trails and enjoyed the intoxicating scents of the damp soil and crushed leaves. The exhilaration of the fresh clear air lifted me spiritually. In the evenings we sat round the log fire and talked about our lives, our hopes and expectations. Here, I found peace.

I thought about Ben. I cared for him. When Isabel died he was a lonely man, lost, for a while, in his grief. There was nothing for me to do, my job had ended but I stayed for a few months to help him over a difficult period. Ben taught me to play chess, and I encouraged him to walk. Each day we wandered to the cemetery. It was not a morbid desire, it was wild and untamed with maple trees and natural woodlands. Ben used to like to sit beside a pond and reflect, and theorize about life, between its beginning or its end and the present.

When the snow disappeared and spring returned I began to think about moving on. The longer I stayed, the more Ben relied on me. We went to a concert in Halifax to celebrate his birthday. We dined in a little place down on the waterfront. The wine, good food and the atmosphere warmed us, followed by the music of Mozart and Vivaldi. When we arrived home I felt the time had come for me to break the news of my imminent departure but I could not destroy his happiness. I waited until we had finished breakfast the following day. I didn't want to leave him, but I knew I had to. "Ben, I have something to tell you." "I think I know what you are going to say," he said. "I have been expecting it; please don't go." Poor Ben! I was saddened for him.

Ben drove me to the bus station. He looked a forlorn figure standing there beside his car, watching the bus pull away, and I, watching him, until the bus turned the corner and we were both left with the memories.

Life Is But
A Game Of Chance

Returning to Vancouver after working my way across Canada, I was about to disembark when to my surprise an arm reached over and picked up my overnight bag from the seat beside me. A man asked where I was going. As I had no plans, I said I didn't know, but thought I would go to White Rock.

He said he would take me, as he lived there. He had been golfing his way around Canada, so he said. It all sounded too improbable but as he was putting my cases into the trunk of his car I could see clubs and other paraphernalia pertaining to his activities.

Surreptitiously I summed him up and decided life was after all, a game of chance. When we reached White Rock, we looked for somewhere for me to stay and found a motel with kitchenette. It was elevated and overlooked the water. Then he left and I did not see him again. To this day I do not know who he was only that he had been my Good Samaritan and lived at Crescent Beach nearby.

On my travels I found reading the local papers provided me with information and insight into the surrounding areas. This was invaluable right across

Canada. So, once settled, I walked down a steep slope towards the waterfront and found a corner store. Buying provisions and a paper I climbed back to my room with a view. Reading the news and scanning the advertisements I read the following notice:

Middle-aged gentleman planning motor trip across Canada and return this summer seeks lady companion, non-smoker, slim, medium height, who enjoys travel, camping, interesting conversation.

I telephoned! We met! We walked, and we talked about ourselves and our lives and discovered we had many mutual interests, which promised well for two strangers planning such an excursion together. We studied books and maps, culminating in a regulated plan. On the fourth day of July we set off on our cross-Canada journey.

Bob, I found to be an excellent companion, an agricultural scientist working with CUSO. There was so much I wanted to know about Canada, the wildlife, fauna and flora, the prairies and crops and Bob knew it all.

I would not describe it as one of the most comfortable periods of my life because we slept in sleeping bags on the ground, in a tent and I was so cold. But it was fun! At night, after a hot supper which I cooked while Bob set up the tent, we sat around the camp fire, drank hot rums, reminisced and listened to music and very often to the hauntingly beautiful cry of the loons. When we reached Waterton Lakes it was pouring with rain and in the middle of the night the tent blew down. I fled to the shelter of the car, my emotions were at low ebb and I wondered how I could have undertaken such a foolhardy adventure, but in the morning I knew my journey had only just begun; the early sun rising above the mountains glistening with new snow and reflecting in the lakes, was a wonder to behold; never in my entire life had I experienced anything so spiritually uplifting. The loons were silenced, but the finches sang in the bushes as clear and sweet as the translucent morning air.

We piled the soaking wet tent and everything else into the car, and set off for Cypress Hill Provincial Park in the middle of the prairies. It seemed incongruous that in this vast, treeless tract of land we would find a lovely camp site amid a forest of whispering aspens, the trees filled with yellow wild canaries that fluttered about like leaves on the wind.

Ten days later we arrived in Montreal and stayed with Bob's daughter and John. They lived in a lovely old home in Westmount. After dinner we climbed Mount Royal, which is the most striking feature of Montreal. It rises in the centre of the city and from the top has a spectacular, panoramic view of the narrow streets and quaint historic architecture that reminded me of a stage that had been set, waiting for the play to begin.

It had been a long day but finally we were shown to our room and slept in the comfort and luxury of a real bed.

The following day the four of us drove to Lake Massawippi near North Hatley, and stayed in John's cottage on the cliff-top overlooking the lake. We swam every day, went snorkelling and sailing. The raccoons and squirrels were so tame they ate out of our hands, and muskrats swam in the water nearby.

There were no near neighbours. The cottage was tucked away in three hundred acres of forest and the beach with its warm, white sand was ours, and ours alone. The trees ran down to the water's edge and provided shade from the hot noonday sun. We swam before breakfast and very often by the light of the moon. Swathed in towels, we scrambled down the cliff trails before stepping into the silken caress of the still water.

Bob and I had been living a carefree and nomadic life, but all of a sudden time was running out. Bob had to return to Vancouver to prepare for his next expedition, this time to Ghana in Africa. Once again we hit the road and camped from one campsite to another until we reached beautiful British Columbia.

Bob and I had travelled countless miles and enjoyed scenic and climatic variables; the colourful prairies with endless crops of golden corn and sunflowers, mixed with fields of blue chicory looking as though a little bit of blue sky had fallen from heaven. We had walked and hiked through rolling hills and enjoyed swimming and sailing, but the time we loved most was sitting round the log fire under the stars, savouring a hot rum, before turning in for the night when the world around us grew quiet and intimate.

It was a chance encounter with unexpected consequences. Bob was a knowledgeable and caring companion who made all these experiences possible. The fond memories will endure forever.

Far From The Madding Crowd

$\mathcal{I}$t was dusk and the loons were calling to one another. Our cabin overlooked the lake; there was a pot-bellied stove in the corner of the room with the wood waiting for the strike of a match. It was wild but comfortable, and I was instantly endeared to the place. This was Nimpo Lake in the heart of the Cariboo country.

We tossed our bags into our cabin and hurried through the woods to the main building for dinner and were met with old-fashioned hospitality, homemade bread fresh from the oven and trout from the lake. Two fires were burning, one at each end of the cabin. There were bookshelves on all the walls; wherever there was a space there were books: novels, reference books, books on fishing and trapping, others telling us about the local area, what to do and where to go and how to do it, and there were easy chairs set around the fires for our enjoyment at the end of the day.

After a good night's sleep we set off on our tour of exploration. Our only means of travel was by plane. Near our cabin was a floating dock made of wood that jutted out into the lake. We flew in a little Cessna or a lumbering Beaver from one lake to another and then hiked. We had packs on our backs and cameras slung around our necks.

There was something magical about flying in a tiny plane over lakes and mountains into the early morning sunrise. The plane seemed flimsy as we rattled our way through the air to Turner Lake; deep and placid as a pond, enfolded in gentle hills of dark green timber running up to white caps of eternal snow. We followed trails through woods leading up to the Hunlen Falls; the morning mist kept swirling through the canyon, mixing with the spray and the roar of the water cascading into the Atnarko River before plunging into Lonesome Lake hundreds of feet below. It was peaceful with the sounds of crackling twigs underfoot, and the occasional chatter of the squirrels. There was a profusion of wild flowers, colourful and varied, toadstools and ferns, but the highlight of the climb was when a grizzly appeared as if from nowhere and shuffled into the bushes nearby.

We flew over the Monarch ice fields to Bella Coola, viewing lakes, which from above looked like blue jewels, interspersed with snow and ice. Bella Coola lay in a valley of incomparable beauty surrounded by almost vertical walls of mountains. Norwegians were the first white settlers, the fjords of the surrounding area reminded them of their native Norway and this is what endeared it to them. Bella Coola was a modern community where Indians and whites lived in relative harmony side-by-side in fishing and forestry. The village consisted of general stores and a post office, churches of all denominations and the Cedar Inn where we stayed and shared our room with a little mouse that came in through the window.

From there we flew with Wilderness Airlines to Ocean Falls, a small logging and fishing village. It was wild and isolated, the terrain so rough the only access routes were by sea and air. Few people live there now but at the turn of the century it was the beginning of a prosperous little town that grew rapidly due to a successful pulp and lumber mill. The community thrived until the Provincial Government bought the mill and soon afterwards declared the machinery obsolete and inadequate, and subsequently closed it.

Ocean Falls has a very wet climate and the people who live there now are known as the 'rain people.' But we were lucky; during the time that we were there the sun shone down upon us with a temperature of ninety degrees.

Where houses once stood the debris had been cleared leaving carpets of flowers, an artistry of pinks and lilacs of the self-sown stocks. What caused Ocean Fall's demise remains uncertain. Maybe it was due to the mill closing, maybe the winter snow-slides that rumbled down the mountains burying homes and apartment blocks causing many deaths. Who is to know? What a story it could tell if only the ghosts of the past could speak.

Last, but not least, we climbed through rain forests to see the Indian petroglyphs, said to be over one thousand years old. We had an Indian guide who scampered from rock to rock like a mountain goat. We were less agile but we all reached our goal.

Nimpo Lake, Bella Coola, and Ocean Falls remain haunting memories. The Cariboo's surreal landscape transcends the rustic cabins and fishing camps. The scenery is a study in contrast from the blue-green lakes and sparse pines, breathtaking rock canyons and river rapids, trout-filled lakes hidden amid the rolling hills, clustered by spruce and whispering aspens to the peaks of the Rainbow Ranges, an astonishing spectrum of reds, oranges, yellows and lavenders.

It was a holiday to remember! Far from the madding crowd, no television, no telephone and no newspapers, just the sounds of the loons, the scent of the forests and the intoxicating air of the High Cariboo country.

Let's Blow Out
The Candles:

When I arrived in Halifax I collected my mail. Having no permanent address, I had arranged for my letters to be held at Post Offices across the country.

Arriving at the YWCA I was shown to my room. I tumbled into bed and slept; sweet rejuvenating sleep. The alarm woke me in time for lunch and as I ate, I read my mail. Freddie, who I had hardly had time to think about, had not forgotten me. Inside the envelope was a Christmas card with a note saying, "I miss you and hope you will soon return to Vancouver." Those words cheered me. The indecision that had plagued me when I left my last job, turned to resolution. I knew what I would do. Suddenly the sun shone. I hurriedly finished my lunch and rushed off to my room.

I began to write:

Freddie dear,

My jobs have kept me busy, no time to think.

I have worked my way from the Pacific to the Atlantic, now is the time to return. Jasper looked inviting as I journeyed eastward and I plan to revisit. I think of you and look forward to our meeting; it seems so long!

A day or two later I left Halifax and commenced my journey Westward. As I neared the Rocky Mountains I had a sense of belonging. I had always loved the mountains, now they embraced me. The train pulled into the station. I stepped on to the platform. Jasper was more beautiful than I could ever have imagined.

I left the station in search of a cab and saw Freddie looking at me. My eyes misted, I thought I was dreaming. For a moment we looked at each other before walking slowly into each other's arms.

"How did you know?" I asked.

"Intuition! I knew you would take the train and I planned to meet each one until you arrived."

We drove into the foothills until we came to a log cabin.

In the centre of the room a fire was burning in a pot-bellied stove.

"Oh, this is wonderful!" I gasped.

"Come," he said, "the talking can wait."

He took my hand and together we climbed the creaking, wooden staircase to the bedroom above. How good it was to be together, the warmth of his body filled me with love. As we lay there in each other's arms we looked through the window at the hoarfrost glistening on the trees running up to the mountain peaks, of eternal snow. I cherished those moments of solitude, alone with my man. I looked at him in wonder and did not speak, I wanted the spell to last forever.

It was hunger that finally drove us downstairs. Freddie put the kettle on to heat the rum, the delicious aroma pervaded the room.

We sat around the fire and Freddie told me, that when my letter arrived he made up his mind to drive to Jasper. On the way he met Tom, who owned a cabin but used it little as his wife disliked the rugged life. He loved it, and did not want to sell, hoping his children would enjoy it when they were old enough. Freddie offered to rent, and a deal was made. "The gods were with me," he said. "I did not expect to be so lucky." The room in which we were sitting had animal skins on the floor, paintings on the walls, pewter pots on the old oaken dresser, and bookcases filled with books. These treasures had belonged to Tom's grandfather, a Dutchman who had immigrated to Canada after the First World War.

Then Freddie began talking about himself:

He, too, was from the Netherlands. "During World War 11 I was an interpreter in Europe," he said, "I took my wife and family to South Africa after I was demobilized, and a few years later we immigrated to Canada. Soon afterwards, my wife died."

"It is strange how circumstances can unexpectedly come to pass. We two Dutchmen met by happy chance, and I have found you," he said.

We talked about ourselves, played records that we had found tucked away amongst the books and the more I heard about Freddie, the more I felt akin to him, from his love of music and reading, to hiking and sailing, a man dear to my own heart and, I knew, the course of my life was about to change. The following day the sun shone more brightly than ever. We pulled on our boots and with cameras and walking sticks, we wandered through the trees and hiked the trails. The forest seemed alive and ethereal. As we climbed we reached a clearing stretching before us. We came upon it unexpectedly and were bewitched by the beauty surrounding us. The woods ran in deep gullies and dropped precipitously into the valley below. The snow magnified the shadows and enhanced the many shades and shapes of the conifers. Suddenly, a cloud covered the sun and the whole scene changed. No longer was it alive and vital but uncanny and fearful. I shivered, although I was not cold. Freddie slipped his arm round my shoulders and we wandered on, leaving behind the profound sense of disquiet that had enveloped us.

We followed the steep mountainside and found a log. After brushing off the snow we sat together and enjoyed our pack lunch while the chipmonks scrounged for food.

The sun peeped fleetingly but soon dipped behind the mountains. Darkness came quickly and clouds began to gather. The high invigorating air renewed our energies, and we hurried back to the sanctity of the log cabin. Freddie stoked up the fire and we talked about dining out, but decided there was enough food in the refrigerator and the cabin was too precious to leave.

We sat round the log fire in the candlelight, savouring the last of the wine while Vivaldi played softly in the background. Then Freddie blew out the candles. "Let's go to bed," he said. "Tomorrow we must leave early." So with hands clasped we climbed the creaking wooden staircase for the last time.